HOLES IN YOUR POCKETS

RACKETS SURVEY

OF

THE NEW YORK COUNTY RACKETS BUREAU

EDWARD R. FINCH, JR., ESQ.

HOLES IN YOUR POCKETS

RACKETS SURVEY
OF
THE NEW YORK COUNTY RACKETS BUREAU

BY

EDWARD R. FINCH, JR., ESQ.

******
****
**

THIRD EDITION

Contributing Authors
Timothy Busler, Esq.
and
Charles Hamilton

PUBLISHER
Edward R. Finch, Jr., Esq.
1993

COPYRIGHT (c) 1941, 1948, 1993 by
Edward R. Finch, Jr., Esq.
Printed in United States of America

Library of Congress Cataloging in Publication Data
HANDS IN YOUR POCKETS
First ed., 1941, has same title
(a) Law Survey of New York County Racket Bureau
Second ed., 1948, has same title
Third ed., 1993, has title "HOLES IN YOUR POCKETS"

ISBN 1-883346-00-2   Hard Cover
ISBN 1-883346-01-0   Paper Trade
ISBN 1-883346-02-9   Video & Movie

Illustrated Publication date - January, 1994

UNCLE SAM - "You are all right, my friend, but who is that behind your back?" - Kirby in the New York Evening Sun.

DEDICATION

TO

RUDY GIULIANI, ESQ.
U.S. ATTORNEY & MAYOR, CITY OF NEW YORK

AND

TO

CHIEF JUSTICE EDWARD R. FINCH
& HIS FRIEND
MAYOR FIORELLO H. LaGUARDIA

Table of Contents

Financial estimate of racketeer levy -
Senate inquiry - levies laid unknowingly
during an average day in Mr. John New
Yorker's life - principal racket case
grouping presented - prominence of
"association"racket types - Lehman orders
rackets investigation - summary.

Extent and interdependence of building trades
- legal complications vulnerability -
background, patterns and Special
Investigation work - general prosecution case
pattern revealed - contemporary cases -
Scalise case - public cases - summary.

What sense minor? - as a training racket
school - minor case groupings - correlation
between certain minor rackets and vital
trucking - minor "association" rackets -
petty governmentals - summary.

TABLE OF CHARTS AND ILLUSTRATIONS

FORWARD
TO 1994 EDITION

The two volumes comprising this work have been reproduced and combined into one volume at the request of several members of the Bar of the State of New York, including Timothy W. Busler, Esq., and of the many friends of the author, including author, Charles Hamilton. The original manuscript was written in 1940 and 1941 prior to the author's graduation from Princeton University. He subsequently was retired from the U. S. Air Force in 1972 as a U.S. Air Force Reserve Judge Advocate Colonel with over 30 years service abroad and in the U.S. He was also a U.S. Special Ambassador and an international lawyer decorated by the Presidents of four countries. The author is now practicing estates, securities and international law in New York City with Snow Becker Krauss P.C.

The updated paperback third edition in one volume comprises the only authoritative analysis of Rackets Bureau cases of the New York County District Attorney's Office for the period 1931 to 1941. The types of racketeering against both labor and management which are shown therein have already recurred in the 1980's and 1990's in many of the large cities of the United States. The current renewed racketeering attempts in the building trades, loan sharking, illegal immigration and the garment industry are examples, of necessary anti-racket enforcement, in tomorrow's free trade world.

This thesis is reproduced with the permission of Princeton University, and abridged from the original two volume thesis for which the author was awarded the Lyman H. Atwater Honor Prize in 1941 by Princeton University. As the author predicted to the Princeton Faculty some fifty years ago, the same patterns of criminal racketeering bringing others hands into your pockets have in fact recurred. Racketeering is now increasing worldwide. Look at Russia! History does repeat itself.

New York City
December, 1993

Acknowledgements

Without the tireless cooperation and thoughtful suggestions of many of the members of District Attorney Thomas E. Dewey's Rackets Bureau of the 1940's this survey and this rackets study never could have been undertaken. To these courageous young men and woman who were then engaged in the endless task of making our City of New York a safe and better place in which to live and to do business, the author is deeply indebted. Through the good offices of Murray I. Gurfein, Esq., then Assistant District Attorney and Chief of the Rackets Bureau full cooperation and full access to published and to source materials on the major rackets was granted, and further to all the members of his then staff the author is also indebted.

Special thanks are due to Mr. Benjamin Margolin, then law librarian, for his numerous leads, suggestions and for reading the manuscript. Also to then Assistant District Attorneys Stanley H. Fuld, (later Chief Judge, New York Supreme Court Appellate Division), Burr F. Coleman, Manuel L. Robbins, and to then Law Investigator George R. Masset, among others, of that office for advice on numerous legal details involved, and to Mr. John F. Cleary for his assistance in locating evasive briefs and records.

Currently, for new recurring factual and legal matters thanks are due for rackets updating materials to Timothy W. Busler, Esq., and to Charles Hamilton, author and graphologist.

Further, the author desires to acknowledge an accumulated indebtedness of several years to the Princeton University Library not only for it's assistance in procuring historical and current periodicals, reports, newspapers, but also for guidance and letters of reference to other libraries. And for more general cooperation, the author desires to thank the staff of the Association of the Bar of the City of New York Library, and the New York Public Library.

Finally, to my wife, Polly Swayze Finch, Miss Ida Miller, Miss Gladys Waldman, Miss Kathryn McHugh, Mrs. Sally Saran and others for their numerous suggestions, untiring secretarial and editing assistance, and for help in collecting records and interview forms, and updating, many thanks.

Cases citations in a majority of instances refer to unprinted court records. Historical references and citations are complete, however, as far as was readily available.

In regard to all statements on persons, companies and other associations in pending and closed cases the author hereby serves notice that he assumes no legal responsibility. Full academic responsibility is, however, assumed as such statements are based on the study of available competent sources of fact and opinion on these rackets cases. In conclusion, the author also assumes full responsibility, for all other statements, and material herein which having been carefully collected, are correct to the best of his knowledge and belief at this writing. History proves rackets repeat themselves.

E.R.F., Jr.

December, 1993

Introduction

As always it is necessary to reach a definition of terms before stating the grounds in any survey. The words "racket," "coercion" and "extortion" have a wide variety of meanings as used in common parlance today. The word "racket" itself is comparatively new but the practice is as old as ancient Greece civilization. Such writers as Raymond Moley speak of caravans being "hi-jacked" in Asia, and Louis Adamic sees rackets in the modern sense arising with the old Irish landlord feuds, and also in the post-Civil War Molly Maguires of the Pennsylvania coal area. In the field of literary masterpieces there also may be seen numerous examples of early rackets, namely in Hugo's <u>Les Miserables,</u> in Gogol's <u>Dead Souls</u>, in Balzac's <u>Les Splendeurs,</u> and in the Waverly novels to mention only a few. But this is not a history of racketeering sources and extortions in any sense. Suffice it to show that we are here dealing with a method as old as civilization itself. It wasn't until the twentieth century, when the new word "racket" became common parlance, that it was attached to the older racketeering methods.[1]

A modern racket may mean anything from door-to-door "sale" of magazines to the literally millions of dollars which once poured into the coffers of Terranova's Unione Scilicano. As long as it is a means of "income," it is a racket in the general sense of the word. There is no exact legal definition. A commonly accepted definition today is:

> "Any scheme by which criminal conspirators live upon the industry of others, maintaining their hold by intimidation, terrorism or political favoritism .. a scheme for easy money, or a blanket definition of organized crime." [2]

---

[1]   Journal of Criminal Law and Criminology, Vol. XXII, Nov. 1931, p. 578.

[2]   This definition by K.O. McCarthy, closely parallels that of John Gunther in The High Cost of Hoodlums. The same may be said for John Landesco's definition of what racketeering is in The Illinois Crime Survey, p. 979.

Origins usually cited for the widespread rise and use of the word in the 1920's are:

(a) An invention of "Big Tim" Murphy's of Chicago.
(b) An invention of an investigator in 1885 who was looting a teamster's union.
(c) An invention of the modern vaudeville stage, having a specialized meaning therein.
(d) An invention of the New York City social political clubs of the 1890's meaning a loud noise party, for which it was found easy to coerce local tradesmen to buy tickets.

In his article in the _Encyclopedia of Social Sciences,_ Murray I. Gurfein makes the further distinction that

> "... it applies to the operation of an illegal business as well as to the illegal operation of a legal business. It cannot be confined to extortions in business alone, for it includes the use of violence to enforce the rules of illegal activities..."[3]

Stated concisely it is then taken to mean the organized extortion of money, sometimes with _apparent_ willingness of the victims by force, deceit, or threats thereof. An additional essential usually found in the Rackets Bureau cases is the presence of the big-shot racketeer or gangster, running his whole racket from remote safety. Witness the John Gotti trial of 1992 and conviction. Formerly he was immune to the law because he himself may not have performed criminal acts and was known only to a few faithful associates. Todays Federal and State rackets and conspiracy laws are much broader! But it cannot be overemphasized that the crimes in the following fourteen chapters were _not_ rackets in any sense, nor did they fall under the jurisdiction of the Rackets Bureau _until_ the gangsters and racketeers

---

[3]   _Encyclopedia of Social Sciences,_ article on "Racketeering," Vol. 13, p. 45.

moved in, organized them, and assumed control, occasionally even monopolistic control. These limitations all apply in large measure to this Rackets Bureau survey which, deals then with industrial racketeering upon both labor and industry except in a few flagrantly then outstanding racket cases.

The restrictions applied to the word "racket" above, apply equally well to the terms "extortion" and "coercion" in regard to their use herein. These latter methods are known to have been practiced in the modern sense both in Chicago and New York City in the early twentieth century, especially in the trucking, clothing and building industries. The stimulus of the first World War and of Prohibition were the food these infant cancers needed so that today their extent is appalling, despite better laws, faster, more accurate and better Federal - State - City racket busting cooperation.

Any attempt to set up a general racket pattern immediately becomes a rule with so many exceptions that the rule itself is swamped. Not only do the criminal racket types vary vertically but as the cases clearly show they have wide horizontal variance from industry to industry. A few of the most common racket patterns which I have evolved by reviewing all prominent New York racket cases of recent years including closed Rackets Bureau cases are:

(a) The monopolist-terrorist middleman rackets.

(b) The direct "protective" association racket.

(c) The indirect "association" rackets with price control and detailed collusive agreements between politicians, labor, business, middlemen and racketeers.

(d) Pure labor rackets involving "kickbacks", "breaking" or "official" extortion of any form.

(e) Pure "business" or lottery rackets involving straight gambling or charity racketeering.

(f) The professional hireable rackets. (Strike Breakers)

(g) The combined "fascist" racket association.

(h) The specialized rackets.

All sometimes employ violence or threats thereof in varying degrees. The New York County Rackets Bureau has to date dealt with all types. Types c, d, g, and h, are most common and sometimes all are combined in what is called a racket hierarchy.

These from the 1930's and 1940's are still in my opinion the main general racket patterns of today. All of these types have been practiced in the City of New York within the past three years.

Working inside these eight general patterns there are two personality types of racketeers, the first is the "parasitical type" and the second is the "stabilizing type." Both, most investigators agree, are a sort of natural growth upon an unbalanced laissez-faire economy, and some will go so far as to say the latter is the personification of economic individualism at its height. The justification for the "stabilizing type"[4] will be briefly considered in a later chapter in the very words of a former racketeer, although of necessity names and places therein are deliberately falsified, and in other cases names are omitted to avoid, libelous statements. The argument as to the evolution of the parasitical and stabilizing types form the basis of a separate investigation and will not be considered in this survey except as a necessary supplement in one instance.

Having now defined the terms to be used herein, it only remains to set the limit of the actual scope of this particular survey. The illegal racket situation in New York City, prior to the founding of the New York County Rackets Bureau on January 1, 1938 at the instance of then District Attorney Thomas E. Dewey, will be briefly reviewed where desirable as background. Then the major phases of the work of that Bureau will be covered step by step through exhaustive

---

[4]   Ibid., p. 46.

investigation of the most typical case in each phase. Using the carefully timed and planned methods of Mr. Dewey this New York City Rackets Bureau, under the able and fearless direction of Assistant District Attorney Murray I. Gurfein and his young assistants, the war on rackets in the greatest city of the world became a deadly, sure, and certain maneuver.

The guiding work of the Rackets Bureau has pointed the pathway to the rest of the cities of this nation for the freeing of the people of America from national bondage estimated at one time as nearly twelve billion dollars annually.[5] That's a lot of racket hands in a lot of people's pockets!

---

[5]   _Infra,_ footnote, p. 9

THOMAS E. DEWEY

Chapter I

The "Unofficial" Sales Tax

Although the Repeal of Prohibition meant happy days for most New Yorkers and temporary release from the doldrums of the 1929 & 1930 Depression, it was far from being happy days in many cases. Hard-bitten groups of men, whose revenues and incomes from the illegal liquor trade had been steadily shrinking largely due to repeal, met together not only in the back alleys of poolrooms, but also in luxurious penthouse apartments, desperately seeking new sources to maintain their revenues. In nine cases out of ten these easy money men turned to business racketeering as the best solution. The other one-tenth turned into out-and-out criminals or else committed suicide as the crime statistics for these years reveal. The result was that the racket bosses of New York became so dollar hungry that they were extorting an "unofficial" sales tax of between thirty-three and eighty-three dollars[6]

---

[6] Consult: Harold Seidman, Louis Adamic, Ruppert Hughes and the Illinois Crime Survey for varying City and national extortion estimates. The exact figures for compiling accurate financial totals are simply unavailable. The Wickersham Committee reached this conclusion also in its investigation at the time.

a year upon every man, woman, and child in the greatest commercial city of the world today.

During the month of August, 1933, the situation had become so acute that a United States Senate sub-committee on racketeering, under Senator Copeland, opened a two-day public hearing in the offices of the Bar Association, 42 W. 44th Street, New York City. Here, among other remedies suggested by public officials were the following: martial law, revival of the public whipping post, stricter firearm control, a new code of public ethics, and the establishment of an "American Scotland Yard." And these in all seriousness by such men as Warden Lawes, Police Commissioner Mulrooney, and Raymond Moley! Election rackets, politics in the Police Department and racket witness timidity were secretly aired. When the New York County Grand Jury had this testimony presented to them by U. S. Attorney C.Z. Medalie, eight days later on August 23, 1933, they not only voted a thorough special investigation but also they rose as a body and made the old musty criminal courts building ring with cheers. Such were their hopes of release from racket bondage.

It was later revealed that some of this extorted money came out of the merchants own pockets, but no one can deny that the majority of costs were shifted down to the consumers in advanced prices, during that Great Depression. Eventually, the organized racket bosses overstepped the mark completely and so brought down upon their well laid schemes a really effective prosecuting campaign that drove most of them to their graves, to the State's prisons, or to other American cities.

The rackets of 1925-1935 were repeated as to racket methods mainly from 1960 to 1970, and again with similar, but more coordinated methods from 1989 to date, proving the racket crime time recidivist methods cycle! How were they able to flourish and grow extensively for almost a decade from 1925 to 1935 exacting literally millions of dollars annually from the poor and rich of New York alike?

Why did the same rackets return from 1960 to 1970? They returned again from 1989 to date! History and criminal rackets patterns do repeat. The story of a few days of the average Mr. John New Yorker of this 1925 to 1935 era best reveals the methods. The actual practical typical case solution will be considered for each major racket category in surveying the work of the New York County Rackets Bureau.

How badly Mr. John New Yorker began to feel all these money extortions may be seen by following this average fellow for one month. John thinks he pays no taxes but he certainly is complaining to Mrs. John about the high prices of the necessities of life for themselves and their children. In addition to the ordinary indirect taxes John pays unknowingly where does the real squeeze come in? The small apartment they live in of five hundred dollars a month really costs them fifty to seventy dollars more than it should. Primary and secondary building rackets on labor was also paying the property tax to support racketeer influenced judges, unprosecuting prosecutors, "blind" detectives and politically-minded cops.

When Mr. John New Yorker arises at his usual hour to go to work he puts on some clean underwear and a clean shirt for the laundering of which he paid an extra price to Owney Madden and his associates.[7] His neatly pressed suit also cost him an extra dollar due to the exactions of Louis (Lepke) Buchalter and his associates. In 1993 it would be at least an extra three dollars.

---

[7] For details see Vol. II, pp. 32ff, 2/28/36, also p. 3, 8/15/33, and The Outlook, May 21, 1930.

At his family breakfast John's toast cost him an extra dime, as did most of the other perishables spread out before him. Here John was supporting Lepke, Jacob (Gurrah) Sharpiro, Herbert (Tootsie) Weiner and a regular racketeers payroll of some three hundred and ninety-five men, depending of course upon the extent of his breakfast tastes. These racket levies were exacted at a series of levels in the manufacturing and handling processes of the food, but mainly by the racket control of the trucking Local 202 and of Local 138, of the Teamsters, Chauffers, and Stablemen's Helpers, by the Flour Truckman's Association, and by the New York Milk Chain Association.

Mr. John New Yorker hurries off to his downtown office _via_ the subway, from which every twentieth nickel was being stolen by the subway agent-collector's racket. While waiting for the subway he buys his morning newspaper from a racket controlled news concessionaire and watches two young public school children lose their luncheon quarters in a racket owned slot machine.

Upon arriving at his downtown subway station John finds he is very late and decides to take a taxi the remaining blocks to his office. In paying this high fare he is contributing to the "honest" graft racket of a member of the New York State Legislature and to the same for the dishonest Commissioner of Motor Vehicles.[8]

After John has been at the office a few hours his wife phones to say she will be down for luncheon with him in their favorite restaurant. Mrs. John New Yorker sets out to do some shopping for some new clothes before lunch. She buys some marked-up lingerie and a "bargain" dress hardly within her means that "she simply couldn't resist." However, she is unable to find a good new fur-collared winter coat within her means. Why? The answer is that the Lepke and Gurrah organizations had an iron-fisted grip not only on several of the main garment and fur workers organizations but also considerable control over the wholesale suppliers, traders and retailers all paying a heavy tribute to them. This raised retail prices 15% to 20%.

At luncheon, Mr. and Mrs. John New Yorker ordered their favorite sea-food dinners as a pleasant change from the eggs and chopped meat of the home diet. When John received the bill he found it higher than usual. Not only has the poor restaurant manager been forced to join the

---

[8]   *i.e.,* Edward S. Moran and Charles A. Harnett.

Metropolitan Restaurant Association under forced strike by Local 16 of the Waiters Union, but also for fear of his own life and the effects of Mully Kramer's shootings or stink bombs upon his food and customers. Further the sea-food dinner costs a little more because Joseph (Socks) Lanza and associates are getting their "cut" from the Fulton Seafood Watchman's and Workers Union. Local 594, and from the Fulton Protective Association.

In all of these combined industrial "association" rackets the real key men remained immune and concealed to the last, even using their director's lieutenants, or controllers to give the orders for dirty work to the underlings who never knew their identity or even the ultimate reason or cause.

When John returned to work in the afternoon, he decided to borrow an extra hundred for his wife's new fur coat, from a small loan broker downtown who "asks no questions and demands no collateral," just his signature and "easy" installment payments. Little did John realize he was ultimately to pay about eighty-five per cent interest on this loan (average for the racket) through these "easy" installments. Mrs. John New Yorker, after a few more hours of futile coat shopping decides to see a new movie before going back to the apartment. The admission price is now one dollar higher because Kaplan, Lepke and Gurrah not only shakedown the movie house manager, for "protection", but also grab off a goodly share of the movie operators, ushers, and distributors salaries mainly through the "control" and high dues of Movie Union Local 306. The only difference is that in this case the racket actually "assisted" the movie house managers by <u>making a complete terroristic monopoly which eliminated effective competition</u>. The same system operated along parallel lines in many of the (fly-by) night clubs of this era.

Upon his arrival at the family apartment John ate a simple supper of soup, spaghetti, tomato sauce, meatballs and a special favorite Italian delicatessen dessert, all of which supported Ciro Terranova and his "crowd" in his luxurious Pelham Manor mansion. And finally, Mr. John New Yorker read his evening paper from a racket controlled news stand,[9] and went to bed with Mrs. John New Yorker whose new negligee has been made in a

---

[9]   The Racket Bureau also investigated certain printing house "charges" and prosecuted as the evidence warranted it. See case citations below p. 196. See also Vol. II, p. 4, Ref. 1/4/34 and p. 6, Ref. 3/31/34.

garment shop which had been forced to pay tribute to Lepke and Gurrah.

Their strong arm men had beaten and murdered the woman manager and several of the jobbers in the garment industry. They received the electric chair, life sentences, without parole, and some were killed in "gang wars."

Even the sleep of Mr. and Mrs. John New Yorker was troubled by the thought of a friend of their errant older son, "the black sheep" of their family, who during the early morning hours could always be persuaded to lend his "pal," a little more of their hard earned money to give to "Lucky" Luciano and his associates for dope, heroin, cocaine or crack or for a lady of the evening.

Such was the situation and "the unofficial sales tax" in the greatest city of the world before the Dewey rackets investigation was ordered by Governor Lehman.[10] What was to be done? The answer will unfold phase by phase in the following chapters.

What you see in those chapters is the successful rackets prosecutions of 1935 to 1940. It was repeated as to criminal racket's patterns and extortions from 1960 to 1970; and again from

---

[10] See Vol. II, pp. 8 and 9.

1989 to date curbed by the addition of some new racket busting techniques. The 1994's continued recession, with lay-offs very common in business, will see organized auto theft racket return, and auto "chop shops" for auto parts and wheels rip-offs. These are old times recurring rackets.

From the slums Ciro Terranova moved to his villa on Pease Street, in Pelham Manor . . .

And Lucky Luciano to the Waldorf-Astoria Hotel

Chapter II

The Building Rackets

The construction company which built the apartment in which Mr. and Mrs. John New Yorker and family live is but a small fly in the cement of the strongly unionized city industries - the building trades. Everything from the $89,999 model home up on the Heights to the then new six hundred million dollar subway system is involved. In fact every structural evidence of urban concentration, both above and below the famous New York skyline, is part of this industry. Here is an enormous union hierarchy made up of a whole multitude of divisions, sub-divisions, local divisions and local sub-divisions. Any one of these whether it be of labor, capital or any government level may stall or stop the whole machine or an interrelated phase thereof, just like the battery in your car.

The legal structure ordinances, rules, and regulations for "the public safety and the common good" fill volumes in themselves for each unit. Even the management of the building industry is in no final way coordinated. The labor unions have their Building Trades Labor Council, it is true, but its powers are as nebulous as the clouds. The plumbing men have their _independent_ trade associations, the electrical workers theirs, the steel workers theirs ---- and so forth, almost indefinitely. Certainly there is little uniformity or coordination of government ordinances, rules and regulations, and the flow and management of capital along with seasonal fluctuations in the various units represents no logically organized or even coordinated picture to the impartial investigator. The temptations in such an enormous, uncoordinated and vital industry for industrial racketeering have never been resisted for one single year in the history of New York City. Certain illegal parasites have and probably will always crop up again in the crucial joints of the necessarily interdependent building trades. Who has the task of keeping such a loose, confused hierarchy in operation, and of preventing the City racketeers from crippling or dominating the whole industry to their own ends? Only a small fearless and courageous group of men and women lawyers in the rackets prosecutions who have the real interest of the People at heart. They must seek out and prosecute the meanest or the greatest of the building trades racketeers and chiselers. They must review in motion and balance the pull and haul of honest labor, capital and government within the vast and divided building industries, to catch criminal rackets early. What has been the record of the New York County Rackets Bureau in the building trades since it was founded on January 1, 1938? How much had it contributed to the total work of the District Attorney's Office and other agencies attempting to prosecute the building racketeers? The first effective continuous effort to correct this situation, aside from previous sporadic prosecutions, began with the start of Mr. Thomas E. Dewey's Special Investigation at the order of Governor Lehman on July 7, 1935.[11] The Rackets Bureau continued and completed much of this original investigation and work then begun. A brief review of the work of the Special Investigation is therefore necessary, especially in regard to the building trades, in order to adequately understand the work of the Rackets Bureau along these lines since it was established.

We have already seen that Mr. John New Yorker of the immediate post '29 Depression years, felt the ever increasing rent demands because of the building racketeers. Thomas C.T. Crain, former District Attorney, said shortly before the Special

---

[11]   See Vol. 2, p. 8, 7/1/35.

Investigation began, "that probably not more than four unions in the whole building trades were free from racketeering."[12]

The first indictment of building racketeers was made on or about January 16, 1936, as a result of the seizure of the books of an A. F. of L. affiliated painters' union, namely the Brotherhood of Decorators, Paperhangers and Painters Local No. 9. Violence at the union's meetings, the results of an internal rift eventually lead Dewey to discover, through arduous and ingenious work, that Philip Zousner had been re-elected as the Local secretary through fraud and racketeering. Members of the Special Investigation including Assistant District Attorneys Priteil and Gurfein, later head of the Rackets Bureau, worked over the records and the defendant was finally brought before the bar; after literally hundreds of union workers had been interviewed.[13] This case is typical of the classic pattern of industrial racketeering as it was uncovered in the notoriously corrupt building

---

[12]   Harold   Seidman,   <u>Labor   czars</u>,   p.   148.
Statement to a reporter of the <u>New York World.</u>

[13]   See   Vol   2,   p.   22,   1/25/36.   For   Justice
McCook's dealings with reluctant witnesses.

trades. Here was a captive labor union ripe for the set-up of a fast growing trade "association."

The most frequent classic example of the building rackets is the case of Robert P. Brindell, one time pal of Mayor Frank Hague's. It was uncovered by Samuel Untermeyer for the Lockwood investigation, many years before the Dewey investigation. The founding of the Rackets Bureau, was two years later.

Robert P. Brindell was a racketeer labor leader and president of the Building Trades Council. For his building trades "extortion" empire he was convicted and given ten years in jail and a heavy fine. With the fall of Brindell and his $1,000 per floor of skyscraper construction extortions, seven trade "associations" were nipped in the bud. These were: the Hoisting Association, the Metal Ceiling Association, the Plumbers Trust Association, the Cut Stone Contractors Association, the Stone Masons Contractors Association, the Masons Supply Bureau and the Eastern Soil Pipe Association. The notorious sporadic prosecutions of the racket empires of Patrick J. Commerford of the New York Building Trades Council and of "Jake the Bum" Wellner, one-time walking delegate of the Painters Unions might well be similarly cited. These cases are only mentioned here to show to what extent the building racket "associations" may be carried by any one man if not immediately prosecuted.[14]

The next phase in the Dewey investigation of the building rackets came when President Bambrick of Local 32B of the building Service Employees International Union advised Dewey that "certain real estate interests" had engaged in a criminal conspiracy against him and his union. This matter is primarily important because for the first time the unions came willingly to the Special Prosecutor and others soon followed suit. Curiously enough there were ulterior motives,[15] then unknown, in Bambrick's appeal to Dewey, but it did serve the purpose of showing certain other really honest union officials that they could go direct to the Special Investigation and get

---

[14] For crime details in these related cases see Seidman, op. cit., pp. 156-165ff.

[15] President Banbrick himself was later indicted by the Rackets Bureau on March 22, 1941 for stealing and racketeering upon real estate men and upon his own Local 32B of the B.S.I.E.U. Dewey stated on March 22, 1941 that the skill and efforts of Assistant District Attorneys Kalpan and Herwitz of the Rackets Bureau "has now finally cleared the international (Building Service Employees International Union) of its worst aspects."

ASK GREEN TO HELP UNION FIGHT GANGS

Painters Specifically Call for Removal of 'Jake the Bum' as Business Agent

PRESTIGE SEEN AS INJURED

Opposition of Realty Men

"We are confronted with incidents where representatives of real estate firms have one reply to all our efforts to organize their properties and that is, 'as long as Jake the Bum is your business agent we will have nothing to do with the painters' union,'" the letter asserted. "The C. I. O., on the other hand, is making an effort to enter the building trades field in Brooklyn and their organizers are using the name of 'Jake the Bum' as a means of keeping away contractors from signing agreements with our union."

In denying the charges, Wellner asserted that members of the majority group in the district council had warned him that he would be "hounded" out of office on the strength of his past record if he did not follow their leadership in the union. He said he had made his comeback in the union in "a legitimate way" and invited reporters to attend a rally to be held tonight at the Brownsville Labor Lyceum, 229 Sackman Street, by his supporters in Locals 860 and 778, the two largest units in the district council.

Despite an agreement with Mayor La Guardia that there would be no tie-up of painting work on the Vladeck housing development on the lower East Side, Louis Weinstock, secretary-treasurer of District Council 9 of the Brotherhood of Painters, Decorators and Paperhangers, ordered 100 painters there to quit work yesterday. They joined 10,000 other striking painters in Manhattan, the Bronx and Staten Island.

Accused Official, Once Jailed for Extortion, Charges a Plot to Oust Him

The leaders of District Council 18 of the Brotherhood of Painters, Decorators and Paperhangers, A. F. of L., announced yesterday that they had asked William Green, president of the American Federation of Labor, to help rid their union of "gangster and racketeering elements."

Through its president, Harry Brustein, and its secretary-treasurer, Sam Freeman, the district council appealed specifically for the removal of Jacob (Jake the Bum) Wellner, business agent of Local 860, who was jailed for extortion in 1937 but who was returned to office in the union's general election last June. The district council comprises six Brooklyn locals, with a combined membership of 3,000 painters.

Reached at the offices of Local 860 last night, Wellner charged that his foes in the council were seeking to oust him because he insisted on a full settlement of the organization's finances and obligations and refused to "play ball" with the Brustein-Freeman administration.

"Jake the Bum," former building trades racketeer now back on the job. A matter which the Racket Bureau watched intently. (Aug. 23, 1940)

effective legal action and freedom from racket control. The prosecutors before then had been compelled to investigate uncooperative and reluctant unions and employers. Gradually union officials and members were becoming aware that their real hope to be rid of the racketeers and hoodlums that preyed on employer and employee alike lay in the Dewey racket investigation, and not in the hopeless District Attorney's office that was completely ham-strung in those days by politics. Business men in the building trades then realized that at last they could get rid of racketeers by their combined testimony and give a court and jury the complete picture instead of simply occasional isolated situations. Witnesses for the prosecution, however, continued to remain exceedingly reluctant due to the widespread terrorism and grip of the racketeers.

As far as the building trades are concerned it was the case of the Ace Brick Corporation, which really struck terror into the building racketeers and started a general racketeer exodus to other American cities as more promising fields than New York. The records show that Dewey "broke" this racket with his usual thunder-clap technique on December 4, 1935. Twelve raids were made simultaneously and the books of some twenty-three firms were subpoenaed at one time. The raids in this three million dollar monopoly occurred in all five boroughs at once and some one hundred witnesses were corralled. The specific racket extortion practiced by this corporation was to force brick lawyers to use Ace trucks and other equipment. Prior to this, building wreckers had received twelve dollars a load for salvaged brick, which then was sold by truckers to builders for fifteen dollars. When the Ace Corporation got their racket in full operation, they forced the wreckers to take six dollars for salvaged brick and then turned around and sold salvaged brick to builders for eighteen dollars. A very neat little three million dollar building monopoly and extortion scheme at the expense of both honest labor and industry! When the Special Investigation cracked this one a good many allied building brick racketeers decided it was time to take a long "vacation."

The next prosecution bombshell which cleared the way showed the repetitive type of work in the building industries that the Rackets Bureau had to prosecute. It was the public contracting cases with the usual collusive bidding, real estate swindle, and construction material swindles, all at the City's expense.

The particular bombshell which brought this type racketeering into prominence was the Buggsy Goldstein case; a public conspiracy-extortion plot with some fourteen other co-conspirator contractors. It had been formed in the labor monopoly of paint and contract jobs for Brooklyn and Queens public school buildings. When this public building racket case type was exploded on or about April 23, 1937, it was revealed that there was one and a half million dollars in the painting end of it alone.

Since then racket cases of this type, especially involving collusive public bidding on City contracting, with money kickbacks are consistently recurring with variations. The record shows that Buggsy Goldstein, Seymour Magoon and the fourteen other racket contractors were found guilty of the above charges on April 8, 1938. All received substantial and varying jail terms. Similar building racketeering recurred vigorously in the late 1980's and early 1990's.

The first building rackets case that Rackets Bureau investigated and handled, with the full cooperation of the District Attorney's Office, was an electrical building contract racket. On or about July 15, 1938 and using the typical planned methodical Dewey technique, the prosecution arrested J. G. Livingston and other officials of his firm[16] and all were indicted for criminal conspiracy. They were also accused of having omitted to make material entries on the books of the electrical contracting corporations involved. Federal income tax prosecution followed. The Dewey law permitting a combined indictment was here utilized as the Rackets Bureau has done on many cases since then. Further details in this particular case never became available as the defendants pleaded guilty. It is mentioned here because of its significance as the first building trades case that came to the Rackets Bureau.

The remaining building trade cases that the Rackets Bureau handled with the exception of one, fall into one or another of the eight types above discussed in relation to the racket's Special Investigation. The outstanding exception is People v Scalise in which an unusual combination of several methods of union extortion were practiced was without the usual "association" front. Instead there was used a quasilegal front which made the common law larceny, the bailee

---

[16] People v Henry Fishback, John G. Livingston, Frank Cooper, et al.

counts, and the forgery counts, go under the guise of inter-union legality.

After months of careful investigation and preparation by the Rackets Bureau, George Scalise and associates of the C.I.O. Building Service Employees International Union were arrested on the criminal counts plus a charge of false pretenses, which later was withdrawn. The difficulty of courtroom proof upon adequate grounds seems to have been the reason Mr. Gurfein withdrew these false pretenses counts before the judge charged the jury. The withdrawal demonstrates the wise policy of the rackets prosecutors to date in only indicting on grounds clearly provable in court without any reasonable doubt. The same wise legal prosecuting tactics are seen in the reduction of the 53 original building trades indictment counts. It is also reflected in the reduction of the specific amounts of extortion from $97,150 to $60,087. It is widely believed, however, that actually more than $1,000,000 dollars in extortion monies passed through Scalise's[17] hands. The prosecutions expert accountant investigator, Mr. A.J. Gutreich, wisely never made such a statement in court. He did, however, uncover the specially

---

[17]   See Vol. II, p. 73, 5/4/40.

marked canceled checks which Scalise received from the B.S.E.I.U. headquarters in Chicago,[18] in the amount of $60,087. to show the jury. Here again are other examples of the thorough evidence preparation the Rackets Bureau used in preparing its criminal rackets cases.

Just before the indictment was handed down by the Rackets Bureau, Scalise was so brazen that he ran for reelection as president of his building service union! He felt secure because he had a checking account made from the monthly take of three and a-half thousand dollars of labor union wages, under the false guise of inter-union earnings for "organization and commission expenses."

Scalise had been given union control of the whole Eastern Territory of the United States, with Pittsburgh and Cincinnati thrown in to boot. When direct criminal evidence showed that Scalise was to "kickback" five hundred dollars of it monthly to other gangsters in official places in the union, then Mr. Gurfein skillfully introduced the "marked" checks into evidence before the jury. The defense never really recovered from this telling

---

[18] Typewritten record of trial in General Sessions p. 2332. Gurfein to Miss Kay (Scalise's secretary) on direct examination.

blow.[19] The best the defendant's attorney could

do against the convincing trial work of Gurfein

and Herwitz was to turn and blame Scheartz on the

GOLD IS CONVICTED IN LABOR RACKET

Bambrick Attends Trial

When the court charged the jurors in the forenoon a group of officers of Local 32B, including President James J. Bambrick, listened intently among the spectators. Gold's lawyer, James D. C. Murray, said he would appeal the conviction.

Gold, who was chairman of District Council 4 of the local, was for the first time since his initial indictment in November with three other officials of the local, placed in a Tombs cell after Judge Wallace had finished his charge.

Previously he had been at liberty in $3,000 bail, furnished by the local. The local, he admitted from the witness chair, also paid the expenses of his trial. Gold gave his address as 57-60 Eighty-eighth Street, Jackson Heights, Queens.

His co-defendants in the first indictment are Robert E. Conroy, 35, of 1420 Grand Concourse, the Bronx, executive director of Local 32B; Manuel Sabarino, 42, of 165 West Eighty-third Street, chairman of Council 8 of the local, and Hyman Palatnick, 32, of 41-36 Fifty-first Street, Woodside, Queens, chairman of Council 2. They are awaiting trial on not-guilty pleas.

Gold extorted the $5,950 from Sydney Claman, a vice president of the Forty-eighth Street Corporation, owner of apartment houses at 685 West End Avenue and 250 West Eighty-fifth Street; Sidney J. Bernstein, a vice president of the Corbell Management Company at $50 Seventh Avenue, operator of an apartment house at 333 West Fifty-seventh Street, and H. Lawrence Herring of Herring & Rosenfeld, operators of the building at 33 West Thirty-first Street, in all of which strikes were threatened since 1937.

Scalise Aide 'Protected' Three Real Estate Concerns From Strikes and Annoyances

EXTORTIONS PUT AT $5,950

Says He Accepted 'Gifts' That Were Forced on Him—Liable to 75 Years on 10 Counts

Frank Gold, 35 years old, an aide of George Scalise in Local 32B of the Building Service Employes International Union of scrubwomen, porters and elevator operators, was found guilty yesterday by a General Sessions jury of eight women and four men, with a woman foreman, of extorting $5,950 in three years from three real estate men. They testified that, through meetings Gold's demands for money, their corporations were spared from strikes, picketing and other labor union annoyances.

'Gold took the witness stand and swore he never threatened strikes nor demanded tribute from the three. He admitted, however, accepting a total of $2,100 from them and further swore it was in the form of "gifts" that they had forced on him.

Judge James Garrett Wallace, after assuring the jurors their verdict was "warranted by the evidence" that had been presented by Assistant District Attorney Victor J. Herwitz, remanded Gold to the Tombs for sentence on March 17.

Gold was convicted on all ten counts in a superseding indictment, returned last December, on each of which he is liable to a State Prison term of seven and one-half to fifteen years, or a total of seventy-five to 150 years. He showed no emotion at the foreman's announcement of the verdict after four hours' deliberation.

Demand Called Customary

They swore that, up to last Summer, Gold threatened strikes and demanded money to stop them as a "customary" practice. In one instance he accepted $1,500 after demanding $2,500. Claman testified he gave $4,300, Bernstein $400 and Herring, $1,250. These payments were made after the granting of favorable union contracts to them, which they signed in their own offices.

Gold surprised the spectators last Friday when he took the witness chair and admitted taking money. He insisted he had been "influenced" by the three into taking money in the form of "gifts." Then he added the total of what he received from Claman was but $500, and not $4,300. He admitted accepting $400 from Bernstein and $1,250 from Herring.

Scalise was president of the international union during the years covered in the trial. He is now serving a State Prison sentence of ten to twenty years as a second offender for stealing the union's funds.

Another revival racket recently prosecuted by the Racket Bureau. (N.Y. Times - 2/26/41)

[19] Westbrook Pegler's column of facts and dangerously libelous opinions on the Scalise investigation was clearly based on the stenographic record. His persistence in keeping the corrupt building union leaders and employers before the New York public (<u>Word Telegram</u>, Mar.-Apr.-May, 1940) materially aided the Racket Bureau's Scalise prosecution and was a postlude to the wave of public indignation the New York press originally had aroused against the flagrantly "rotten" loan shark rackets. (See ch. 7, p. 86.)

racket extortion charges. Even Scalise decided to quit in the union re-election, "in loyalty to the union."

But the Rackets Bureau was not satisfied simply to catch one big building racketeer with his hands in the union working man's pockets. They quickly extended the investigation into the affairs of other building unions. Members of the detective staff went right into a union convention. There they subpoenaed other ranking union officials as material witnesses. With the new evidence thus acquired they indicted other "suspicious building officials on a conspiracy charge,"[20] even before the Scalise case was completed. Thus the Eastern Territory of the United States in the Building Service Unions was fast being cleared of these racketeers by the effective and painstaking work of the Rackets Bureau.

While Mr. Gurfein and three of his assistants ceaselessly pushed forward this good work in the building rackets, another assistant prosecutor was preparing a routine City contract "padding case" leading to the indictment of three men who

---

[20] For example: People v Isidore Schwartz, Louis Schwartz.

defrauded the City of $14,959 on two building projects. This is the typical New York County Racket Bureau work since it's founding on January 1, 1938, in clearing and in trying to keep the City's building trades and its unions clean of criminal racketeering. Now in the 1990's there is excellent Federal and City cooperation in the investigation and prosecution of building rackets.

Chapter III

The Minor Rackets

Mr. John New Yorker's morning move was to reach for a clean shirt and his neatly pressed suit. Here we find ourselves involved not only in the cleaning, pressing and laundry rackets but also in a maze of minor rackets which deal largely with the so-called personal service industries.[21] The principal minor rackets with which the Rackets Bureau then dealt are included in this chapter. They are only minor rackets in the financial and temporal sense. These are mainly the press "good story," rackets which are consistently over-emphasized by the daily media.

The minor rackets, considered as a whole, are important because they are the basic units from which the larger rackets hierarchies inevitably grow. The testimony of many of the Rackets Bureau's minor cases clearly show that they are the training school for big professional racketeers. As a matter of fact, in one case[22]

---

[21]   For a complete classification of Recent Metropolitan Rackets see Appendix A, p. 192.

[22]   People v. Elia et al.

there was organized as an integral part of a hierarchy a minor racket called "a school for sabotage,"[23] in which the means for the most effective sabotage persuasion methods were taught in special classes. The Illinois Crime Survey also notes several such schools operating at one time in the City of Chicago.

There was an interesting group of permanent minor racketeers. They are exceptions to the general group for which the minor rackets on the whole served as the necessary training school. The minors group seemed to have no desire to branch out into the big rackets, and big money; or to combine with any big racket hierarchy for high, percentage cuts and kick-backs. It was a curious varied industrial racket group in every respect. Dopey Benny Fein was the leader. There was hardly a decent strike during the 1930's and 1940's in which Dopey Benny did not enlist his sluggers on one side, or the other; and sometimes for both labor and capital at once! But he and his group were permanent pikers for they only collected small money. It never crossed their mind that

---

[23] People v. Rubin Wassage, Sol Freedman, Anthony Serrano et al, 1939.

they could easily be the racket boss of those men and industries who "employed" them!

A brief paragraph on the main trends in the most important of the minor rackets will shed far more light on the minor metropolitan racket field.

The laundry, cleaning and pressing rackets have been some of the most persistent and troublesome of the whole minor group. A prominent New York justice who refused to allow his name to be used in this connection told me that he personally felt the main reason lay in its necessarily intimate connection with the local trucking industry. Obviously the control of such a vital industry is the key to the pot of gold sought by every metropolitan racketeer.[24]

The trend in most of the minor rackets, like the laundry rackets, appears to be away from such relatively simple independent forms as straight extortion and "protection."[25] The present trend is toward the "association" type, described above, of which the "Affiliated Laundry Owners Club" is a

---

[24] See Ch. V. "The Transportation Rackets," p. 62

[25] i.e., Racket cases of types a and b have only occasionally recurred since 1935. Trend is toward types c to h. (Reference to Introduction pp.8 and 9.)

typical example.[26]   The racketeering in the laundry, cleaning and pressing industries had been largely due to the exacting work of Leon Scharf and his crooked Metropolitan Cleaners and Dyers Association.   Here is the usual "association" racket structure;[27] only in this instance the whole extortion structure was just one little cog in a complete network of rackets controlled by Lepke and Gurrah. Owney Madden operated another New York Laundry racket under a similar type of cover, and in the specialized cleaning and pressing fields Louis (Lepke) Buchalter developed several other evanescent "association" fronts.

The correlation between the degree of dependency of a small business and the degree of necessity of trucking delivery services to the business existence was a key to the extent of its racket susceptibility. The testimony of cases in the cosmetics, merchandise, furniture, liquor, oil, coal, newsstand and in the other minor service industries clearly indicates the extent and validity of such a tied-to-trucking racket to survival correlation.

---

[26]   Consult People v Edward Lollo, Jacob Mellon, Morris Rosenberg.

[27]   _i.e.,_ Type c. (Reference to Introduction p.6)

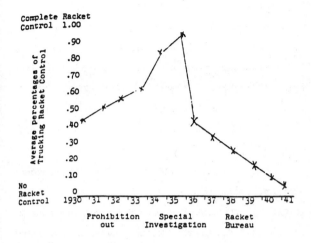

Compound Correlation Curve between the degree of dependency of certain small businesses and the degree of necessity of trucking service to its existence as a key to its racket susceptibility. (A combination of the specific curves by years and cases for the minor industries noted in the above.)

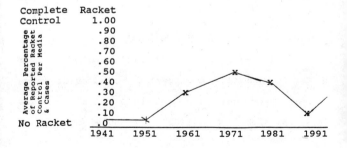

Between 1931 and 1935 when numerous minor rackets were especially rampant, the New York Department of Finance reported that some 140 industries has been compelled by the organized criminal rackets to leave the City. In the 1990's business leaves the core of cities because of graft and excessive urban bureaucracy, excessive ordinances, excessive small business City taxation, and excessive State and City tough ordinances and regulations. When profit margins in Cities fall drastically, the racketeers move to the wealthy suburbs. Minor business and labor racketeering in the late 1920's had grown so common and extensive that these small businesses simply could not be operated at a profit.[28] The then correlation shows a steady increase until the beginning of the Special Investigation of rackets in 1934 under Thomas E. Dewey began to take effect. By December, 1935, many of the minor racketeers saw the handwriting on the wall and they it was who started to leave town instead of the businesses. A happy reversal indeed! From this point on the racket to survival business correlation in the 1940's and 1950's steadily

---

[28] The Murphy report states: "138 firms left because of human parasites'." Special Report for the N. Y. Dept. of Finance, 1935.

Inquiry In Milk Racket Holds Bernoff

Reputed Lepke-Gurrah Aid Put Under $50,000 Bail; Case Called Biggest Yet

Jacob Bernoff, known in the underworld as "Jewie Cohen," was held in $50,000 bail yesterday as a material witness after District Attorney Thomas E. Dewey described him as one of the principal figures in the milk racket, the latest major racket to come under Mr. Dewey's scrutiny. The District Attorney also said that Bernoff was the man whom Louis ("Lepke") Buchalter and Jacob ("Gurrah") Shapiro left in charge of their racketeering enterprises in New York when they became fugitives in 1937.

Bernoff's arrest yesterday by Acting Lieut. William J. Grafnecker and two other detectives and an investigator, all of Mr. Dewey's office, at Sixth Avenue and Fifty-seventh Street, was described at Mr. Dewey's office as the first big break in the milk racket investigation, which, Mr. Dewey said, had been going on for seven months.

According to an affidavit filed by Bernard Yarrow, Assistant District Attorney, with Judge Saul S. Streit, in General Sessions, who fixed Bernoff's bail, the milk racket has flourished "since the beginning of the year 1935 to the present day." The affidavit added that "during the course of this racket, many large extortions of money from business men in the milk industry have taken place."

Revival of Larry Fay Racket

The racket was a revival of the one which the late Larry Fay conducted in the milk industry before his trial and acquittal in General Sessions in 1931, with sixty-two co-defendants. Fay, who was murdered on New Year's Day, 1935, shook down scores of dealers in loose milk by forcing them to join an employers' association. In the current racket, the extortions have been accomplished without the use of such an association, investigators explained.

At Mr. Dewey's office the milk racket was described as the biggest yet uncovered, even surpassing the restaurant, prostitution, numbers, flour-trucking and garment rackets. However, few details of its operations have been disclosed.

Jacob Bernoff, committed yesterday when he failed to raise $50,000 bail.

Times Wide World

Few Details Are Provided

Mr. Dewey did not disclose any details of the racketeering, not even to say whether it was confined to the loose milk business, as had been previously reported. He admitted the capture of Bernoff had been planned for more than two months by Assistant District Attorney Aaron Benenson, Mr. Yarrow and Lieutenant Graefnecker, and expressed elation over what he declared was the most important development up to date in the investigation.

Mr. Yarrow revealed before Judge Streit, however, from an affidavit he read to the court, that Bernoff's testimony was needed before the grand jury as "material and necessary" in connection with evidence that Mr. Benenson recently had uncovered against several "prospective defendants" in the racketeering. He also said that Bernoff, on learning in 1938 through some mysterious channel that Mr. Dewey had started to delve into that racket, had vanished, but even so remained in close touch ever since with others of his alleged confederates in the manipulation of the racket.

He added that when Mr. Benenson and the detectives put renewed pressure about two months ago in their hunt for Bernoff, there had been recent startling developments before the grand jurors which made the presence of Bernoff before the body most necessary.

He further declared to Judge Streit that Bernoff had been disclosed as having been a principal in regular conference among the racketeer leaders and others, whom Mr. Yarrow's auditors assumed to mean victims, all through the twelve years of the racketeering in the milk industry, and insisted that, although he knew that Bernoff could raise $75,000 bail with ease, he was not certain Bernoff would not sacrifice that amount to bail rather than appear before the grand jurors.

Another revival racket nipped in bud by the Racket Bureau. (Jan.3, 1941)

-45-

declines. As each new case was then "broken," all the allied minor racketeers would "fade out" fast. Finally, this correlation reaches nearly zero when Murray I. Gurfein and the Rackets Bureau began keeping a steady watch on the infamous Local 202 of the Teamsters Union while destroying the other rackets slowly but surely.

Other important groups in the minor rackets are the graft and petty governmental rackets. Recent examples are: the broker's racket, the Civil Service Rackets, the customs rackets, the draft card racket, the elevator inspection racket, the gasoline racket, the immigration, passport and naturalization rackets, the job resume and placement racket, the relief vouchers racket, the sales tax racket and the several license rackets, to mention only a few. Petty governmental rackets, which have been the worst repeaters in the 1990's, are the bail bond rackets, the welfare, and the immigration forgery rackets. The common criminal case is still one of "fees and bribes as a public officer." They recur regularly from 1930's to the 1990's. Consider the temptations of an unemployment or welfare benefits reviewer. Strict computer controls only partially save the day! Separately they seem trivial but in the aggregate they represent a tremendous financial drain on local metropolitan State and Federal governments, and a permanent "headache" to all the rackets prosecutors.

A typical government type racket case is the marriage racket.[29] In the late 1930's Deputy City Clerk James H. McCormick was in charge of the New York City Marriage Bureau in the Municipal Building.   He ran the chapel there as a bridegroom's shakedown for some $222 each and did that to 388 people before his "romantic pinknail" was busted and he paid a heavy fine plus four months in jail. Many of the minor governmental rackets resemble this one in two respects. They are ordinarily independent, isolated instances and secondly most have a shield of false legality cloaked around them, as did this marriage license shakedown.

No survey of the minor rackets handled by the Bureau is complete without a word on the case of Dominic Tossone. This 1940's case, in Mr. Dewey's words is "petty but typical of all New York City racketeering." It seems that Dominic extorted five dollars per month to protect apartment house windows from being broken. Dewey directed an apartment house owner to pay the money and caught

---

[29]   People v James J. McCormick.

-47-

Dominic. After they proved Dominic had also been in a petty larceny and in a purse snatching charge, they recommended a suspended sentence after giving the young man a good scare. Certainly a petty extortion but one which shows that the chief prosecutor and his Rackets Bureau director were exercising excellent criminal psychology in the handling of minor racket defendants.

Here in the records is a raft of human interest racketeering material that is fine for literary work but hardly for an analytical survey. It is the ingenuity displayed in the operational schemes and workings of many of the minor rackets along with the detection and prosecution thereof, that makes these minor isolated racket cases especially fascinating. Much of this testimony reads like a novel. It's only real analytical usefulness might be for study of types of specialized minor racketeering methods.

Chapter IV

The Perishable Foods Rackets

It will be recalled that the New Yorker family at breakfast were supporting a number of racketeers who extorted not one, but several levies at different stages on nearly every article of perishable food Mr. John New Yorker had purchased. Their breakfast this morning consisted of the usual fare of fruit, toast, butter, eggs, milk and/or coffee, with perhaps a slice of chicken slipped between two pieces of bread for Johnny's luncheon sandwich at school that day.

This simple, everyday breakfast is composed entirely of perishable foods, the key to which in any city is the control of the trucking industry, from the very fact that they are highly perishable. The rackets to survival correlation curve which was carefully evolved above covered a full period of ten years. Certain minor rackets here follow the same development, but break downwards more sharply than the others during the early months of 1938 and 1940 especially. The reason is that during these months the Rackets Bureau's investigations in these fields caused considerable curtailment of certain rackets as they reached a climax shortly before the indictments were returned. The indictment dates in the cases of People $\underline{v}$ Waldorf, People $\underline{v}$ Manganaro and of People $\underline{v}$ Elin, Persico, Schuster, Zaientz, Polemni, Iannoconne et al represent the heaviest dips in the trucking-perishable foodstuffs correlation curve. The lasting effects of the work of the Racket Bureau only begins to appear as a continued low correlation for the last half of the year 1939 and for the years 1940 and 1941. This happy situation for the City's millions of consumers promised to continue as long as the District Attorney Rackets Bureau prosecutors maintained their vigilance in the City's comparative price indexes and perishable food industries. In the 1990's new prosecution methods with electronics and intergovernment coordination, plus large and fast data bases help control racketeering today. Speedy investigation media reporting in the 1990's has also helped.

The trucking side of this rackets to business survival correlation for the perishable foodstuffs will be discussed in Chapter V on the Transportation Rackets. Here we shall deal with the type, extent, and remedy used for solving the rackets trucking problem in each perishable food item the New Yorkers had on their breakfast table.

First, there are a group of perishable food rackets mainly dealing with the handling and shipping thereof which are clearly in the twilight zone between legality and illegality. These usually turn out to be Federal cases falling under the interstate commerce laws or the anti-trust laws, especially in the fruit, milk, egg, vegetables, and poultry industries which have been the worst Federal offenders.

These recurring coordinated Federal anti-racketeering drives grew out of a U.S. Senate public hearing into New York's racketeering, held in the Bar Association Offices on August 14th, and 15th, 1933. As a result of Senator Copeland's recommendations the Federal anti-racketeering drive was started in the City and coordinated its work with that of the District Attorney and the Rackets Bureau to the advantage of both. These cases which are largely Federal do not, of course, properly belong in the survey of work and jurisdiction of the New York County Rackets Bureau. Sometimes, however, the work of the one points to the other. Here as always it is difficult to tell which activated the other to investigate in a given city industry. It is like the proverbial riddle of which came first, the chicken or the egg. Take your choice.

Before turning to the fruit rackets, we come face to face with the markets problems for perishable foods in Greater New York. The District Attorney's Office was compelled to handle many market cases in perishable foodstuffs involving minor coercion and extortions until Mayor LaGuardia and Commissioner Morgan decided to clean up the markets in 1938.

There is physical evidence of the thoroughness of the clean-up produced here not only in the sharp reduction of the number of minor cases in the perishable foods but in the far better conditions one may see in 1994 in the Harlem fruit and vegetable market and in the licensed Village open-air markets.

The most extensive racket case in the fruit industries has been an "association racket."[30] The racket structure here is very similar to the conspiracy "association" rackets we have already seen in the building trades. Only the operating methods were different.

A brief glimpse at the abbreviated form of indictment used in People v Manganaro, a typical fruit racket case will reveal the extortion structure employed here, and further will present

---

[30]   People v Albert Manganaro (Al Ross).

a concise picture of a typical Rackets Bureau indictment.

The six count streamlined "Dewey indictment"[31] handed down by the Rackets Bureau on June 15, 1937 charged "...... The crime of Extortion committed as follows ...... from on or about April 19, 1937 the above named defendant in the said County of New York, feloniously, wrongfully, and extorsively obtained the sum of ...... (Specific amount)...... lawful currency of the United States of America, the property of .... (name of agent, officer, employee)........ of the .... (Level Fruit Merchants Association, Inc.......... from an officer, agent and employee thereof with his consent by the wrongful use of force and fear, induced by threats of said defendant ....(Level Fruit Merchants Association Inc.)....... for the purpose of the private advantage and gain of said defendant and not with the purpose of bettering the working conditions and wages of their

---

[31] An abbreviated combined indictment developed for the use of all bureaus in the New York County District Attorney's Office by Stanley H. Fuld, Chief of the Appeals Bureau. Its form has been highly praised as "a great contribution to the expedition of the machinery of justice" by members of the Faculty of the Harvard Law School.

employees, and to unlawfully and forcibly restrict and prevent the trucks of the members of said ....(Level Fruit Merchants Association, Inc.) .... from being loaded with fruits and vegetables in the markets of the City of New York, said loading of their trucks being a necessary condition and requisite to the carrying on of the business of said members of the ....(Level Fruit Merchants Association, Inc.) ...."

The second count is in the same form except that the sum and instance of extortion is different. The third count is also similar except here Adolph Peltz and Maurice Peltz are named as those upon whom the extortion was perpetrated. In the fourth count a strike among the Peltz employees was extorsively threatened, and in the fifth count another specific sum was extorted. In the sixth count the sum was extorted from Leiman Brothers, then truckers of perishables.

"..........All of the acts and transactions alleged in each of the several counts of this indictment are connected together and constitute parts of a common scheme and plan."[32]

This is a very brief summary of a six count indictment in an average Racket Bureau case. Something of the magnitude of the work on each count can be understood when we realize that _each_ specific instance had to be detected, investigated, prosecuted, and supported throughout the trial and subsequent appeals. Small wonder the racketeer defendants today dislike the "Dewey indictments"[33] and the Dewey Joinder Law permitting combined counts against several defendants at once! On the other hand, the racketeers had plenty of your money and my money, in fact _every City consumers money_, with which to hire the best defense attorneys available for their trials and appeals. Therefore the Rackets

---

[32] Indictment No. 220876 - General Sessions, County of New York, p. 4ff.

[33] The 54 count indictment in the Scalise case (see Ch. II, p. 20, People v Scalise) was presented, and so the 90 count indict-ment in the Luciano case was presented (See Ch. XI, p. 145 People v Luciano.) The pertinent material in even the lengthy new "streamline" indictments has been summarized in discussing the typical cases within each racket grouping. The above Manganaro indictment has been selected as illustrative of the usual extortion racket form in common use by the Rackets Bureau.

Bureau's trials were often hotly contested, long, drawn out legal battles,[34] as was the situation in the Manganaro perishable foods case. The Federal RICO Act has expanded wisely the early Dewey Joinder Law indictment process.

An analysis of the testimony shows that the main defendants here were the secretary-treasurer and walking delegate of a union local which handled highly perishable fruits and vegetables. Without even using a subordinate as a "front," Manganero went out in his capacity as a union official and extorted money from the very people and produce concerns that he, on behalf of his own men, had to make contracts for wages and hours. Such middlemen and retailers as the Level Fruit Merchants Association, Inc., had as members were highly vulnerable prey for Manganaro. A strike or sabotage for even one day or night by the honest working men in Manganro's local union or a word from him meant a loss of thousands of dollars to these dealers in spoiled fruits and vegetables.

Manganaro didn't even seem to care what the men in his union required or what they deserved.

---

[34] Trial and technique methods and statistical summary of results including the methods of selecting cases, is discussed in detail in Chapters XI and XII.

For example, in one situation he met an honest dealer of the Level Fruit Merchant's Association, Inc., in the Susquehanna Bar and Grill and threatened to pull his union out on strike unless he was bribed $2,500 not to do it. The union workers would have starved and the produce spoiled if Peltz had not finally paid him $1,750 mostly out of his own small business account. This small racket was worked regularly for some nineteen months on various dealers and merchants. Such was the set-up in the fruit and vegetable industries until the Rackets Bureau stepped in.

Turning immediately to the milk industry we find much the same situation, except here the rackets were, and are today, far more cleverly concealed, mainly because the Federal agents and the State Health Department were watching the troublesome milk industries and shipments. One racket unit in the milk industries was a section of the notorious Lepke and Gurrah hierarchy. A typical instance here, however, is the racket Larry Fay organized that boosted the price of the City's milk bill almost $9,000 per day. There were 91 independent members in the Milk Chain Association before this milk racket was finally cleaned up to the delight of both the Borden and the Sheffield Companies. They were beginning to fear that soon every independent milk dealer in the City, would be in a united racket monopoly aimed at destroying the legitimate milk business they operated. It was revealed that these racketeers even had the New York City Health Department under "control" for a short time. In recent years, however, most of the real trouble in the milk industries has been legitimate labor trouble,[35] price non-competition monopoly, and not racketeering.

In the flour, bakery and bread industries we come face-to-face with the most notorious racketeers in the City of New York; namely, Louis (Lepke) Buchalter and Jacob (Gurrah) Sharpiro.[36] Their rackets in the bread and allied industries were but a small part of a large racket empire of which we have already seen a portion in the minor rackets. The Chief Lepke and Gurrah lieutenant in

---

[35] For legitimate labor troubles in the milk industry see "The Milk Industry in Politics in N.Y. State," Harold A. Jerry, Princeton, '41.

[36] Consult: People v Louis Buchalter, Max Silverman, Harold Silverman, and Samuel Schorr Record on Appeal, Vol. III, pp. 1440-2170, for a brief summary of their total criminal activities.

the bread industries was one Max Silverman. Some of the Lepke and Gurrah gunmen murdered William Snyder,[37] President of Local 138 of the Teamsters Union. Silverman had the flourmen, bakers, jobbers and truckers in a neat little arrangement. He formed under him a perfect "association" racket hierarchy coordinated in the United Flour Truckmens Association, of which he was the president and treasurer. Into this he forced the formerly legal N. Y. Flour Trucking and the Brooklyn Flour Trucking Associations. Next had come the jobbers and just as he predicted "next will be the bakers." This occurred only after a long reign of terror in which men were beaten, trucks overturned or set afire, and motors "conked" permanently. The bread rackets grew to such proportions that Lepke and Gurrah had to hire a lawyer, Benjamin Spevack, to help Silverman keep the racket properly "under cover." The luxurious combined Association offices were located at 111

---

[37] The Snyder murder case was eventually solved by District Attorney Dewey when Mrs. Snyder appealed personally to him. The Rackets Bureau conducted most of the investigating and trial work which lead to the indictment of Morris and "Wolfie" Goldis, for this union murder.

Broadway.[38] Small wonder the New Yorker family were then paying a high price for their bread and rolls!

The steps which the Special Investigation and the Rackets Bureau took to correct this particular situation involve a series of careful and methodic investigations and prosecution which finally lead to the top of the hierarchy with the combined indictment of Lepke and Gurrah along with Max Silverman, and others, on October 27, 1937. The racket structure in the bread and allied industries rapidly collapsed, and a good many of these racketeers went into hiding and became fugitives. The drive against many of these racketeers continued and became part of the main work of the Rackets Bureau. It was not until the end of February, 1940 when the Supreme Court Appellate Division First Department[39] reviewed the

---

[38] Total extortion figures for the bread industries are frankly only estimates, as there never were any "association" books kept. Those that were are obviously, so altered, padded and crooked by association officials that they make very little real sense. Estimates vary from $1,500,000 to $2,800,000 yearly.

[39] People v Louis (Lepke) Buchalter, Max Silverman, Harold Silverman (Defendants-Appellants) and Samuel Schorr (Defendant.) Supreme Court Appellate Division First Department.

decisions of General Sessions that these racket leaders were finally convicted for their part in the flour and baking industries. Lepke was sentenced on 14 counts and committed to "State's prison for a minimum term of 30 years, the maximum to be his natural life."[40] Only then did it finally appear that the bread and allied industries were to be at last comparatively free from industrial criminal racketeering.

The rackets in the butter and egg field follow the general survival to racket control correlation curve already noted with only minor variations. The main clean-up here came when a _Federal_ jury indicted 15 persons in the dairy rackets on January 16, 1936. A three firm conspiracy netting $300,000 yearly had been uncovered. Besides the Racket Bureau's vigilance in these City industries, Prosecutor Amen of Brooklyn and other Federal grand juries of recent years have done the most active work in clearing, and in keeping clear, the butter and egg, milk and cheese, perishables from trucking racketeering. Perishables trucking is very often interstate and thus Federal. In 1930's and 1940's the New York

---

[40] _Ibid_., Paragraph 6444, _Record on Appeal_, Vol. III, Now again pending on higher appeal.

City Rackets Bureau itself, had not been compelled to hand down any indictments in the butter and egg industries.

But the slice of chicken that went into young Johnny's sandwich for school is a very different story. Here we are dealing with a large notoriously corrupt industry and one which then had and has had since far reaching repercussions. [41] In 1940's years the Weiner brothers, Herbert and Joey, along with Charles (Tootsie) Herbert were the worst offenders. They organized a racket "association" hierarchy that covered eventually almost every aspect of the industry, and their control was an air-tight structure enforced for a number of years by the usual coercion methods. Their main "associations" were the Metropolitan Feed Co., the New York Live Poultry Trucking Company, the New Jersey Coop Company, the S.S. and B. Live Poultry Chamber of Commerce. They also had the distributors and dealers well in hand, so that they not only held official positions in these, and many of the employers' groups, but also held official positions as representatives of the

---

[41]   Vol. II, p.6 4/20/34.

workers in the several unions. Tootsie Herbert,[42] for example, found the chickens so lucrative that he was at one time drawing several thousands dollars a week and was head man in a $100,000,000 industry. He often gave as much as $50,000 to Bronx charity and had special hair pomade, rafts of $800 suits and a $40,000 automobile presented by his union members. When he went on trial they were assessed $50 per man from their wages to help protect the man who was "saving" the poultry industry!

As an opening wedge in cracking the poultry racket in 1935, taxes were the chief weapon against these "association" racket structures which had a ninety per cent monopoly on the distribution of poultry in the City area. But the New York County District Attorneys's Office eventually caught up with these racketeers again in 1937, after their first jail stretch "up the river." This time the poultry rackets were really "busted" for several of the principal defendants pleaded guilty after they heard the testimony the office had piled up against them. Such was the situation in the poultry racket. No extensive

---

[42]   For specific charges see Vol. II, P. 27, 8/4/34; p. 30, 1/5/37 and 37, 7/28/37.

difficulties were reported in the 1940's, and the work of Commissioner William F. Morgan and Mayor LaGuardia in connection with the markets clean-up had of course been a principle factor in keeping the poultry rackets at their 1940's low ebb.

No survey of their City's perishable foods rackets would be complete without delving into the terrible stench of the fish rackets. Racketeering in the fish industries had nearly as bad a record as that in the poultry industries, beginning back in 1919!

Minor Rackets operated sporadically in the fish industries until 1920 when the notorious Joseph (Socks) Lanza recognized the possibilities and started to coordinate the fish racket structure. Although on the surface, the numerous small extortions Socks made, appear not to be very great, yet actually they were, for Socks soon was "working" on almost every transaction in a quarter of a billion dollar City fish industry. He was typical of most racketeer leaders in that he rose from the City slums on his own initiative; but different in that he remained a genuinely popular representative for a good many small seafood dealers. Socks was thus more a trade representative of his fish unions than many of his racketeer contemporaries in other industries; but he did often extort monies, just as much from his unions, as from the fish captains, wholesalers, dealers, and City retailers!

There again, the usual trade "associations" were organized, namely, the Fish Credit Association, the Fulton Fish Market Association, the Bronx and Upper Manhattan Fish Dealers" Association, Inc., the Brooklyn Fish Dealers Association and the United Seafood Workers Union, Local 594, A. F. of L. affiliated. District Attorney Crain, of New York County, indicted Socks on a small charge in 1933, but Socks easily escaped the lower Court "information" due to the influence and protection of then City Hall - Tammany politics. Shortly thereafter, however in 1934, the <u>Federal</u> agents and prosecutors under Medalie put Socks "on the carpet" for his activities. Here the result was very different. Socks served two years in jail and paid a $10,000 fine, but only after a close fight with Commissioner William F. Morgan to see who was the real boss of the fish markets.[43]

While Socks was in jail, he continued to hold his union position and to draw his several

---

[43] See Vol. II, p. 3, 5/7/33. also p. 19, 12/4/35; p.20, 12/28/35; p. 74, 8/1/40 and p. 75. 8/2/40.

"salaries." Upon release in 1935 he was welcomed back in great style and it wasn't long before he had the whole racket operating again, except this time a little better concealed. Socks was warned in several instances and remained exceedingly cautious. Finally, he overstepped the traces. After a careful investigation and collection of material and witnesses he was reindicted, along with two henchman, by the Rackets Bureau on July 31, 1940. [44] Being a repeat offender Socks was of course dealt out a considerably longer jail term this time. Earlier in the year, the A.F. of L., in cooperation with Mr. Dewey's Rackets Bureau saw that Local 594 had not heeded his former warning as to the re-election of Socks. Dewey suspected all along that Socks had been "tampering" with union funds. The charter was returned when the Local elected another man to take Sock's offices, due to his reindictment and "compulsory resignation for the good of the union," to use his own words in the courtroom.

Having now reviewed the major work of the Rackets Bureau in the perishable foods industries let us turn at once to the other part of the vertical side of the correlation; namely, the

---

[44]   People v Joseph (Socks) Lanza et al.

trucking and transportation industries, which we have already seen are so vital a control factor in many of the City's most important perishables industries.

Consider the main perishable foods found in Mr. John New Yorker's small refrigerator and for the breakfast meal spread on the table before the family. No wonder neither John nor his wife could explain very readily why their food bills had each month become rapidly much higher. Certainly it was not inflation then at 2%. John felt that perhaps his wife was growing a bit wasteful of late, but like most "patient" husbands he made up his mind very wisely to "stay out" of the food costs! So he grabbed his hat and coat, kissed little Johnny and his wife, and dashed off for the subway to his office.

DAILY NEWS, THURSDAY, JANUARY 9, 1941

SOCKS LANZA'S CHARM FAILS, HELD IN 'SHAKE'

By John Martin and Jack Turcott.

Two decades of apparent immunity from the laws of New York ended yesterday for Joseph (Socks) Lanza, leader of a gang of waterfront gorillas and racket dictator of the city's food industry.

The pudgy racketeer was arrested at 9:45 A. M. yesterday at his headquarters in Meyer's Hotel, 119 South St., by District Attorney Dewey's detectives. He was charged with extorting money from labor unions by threatening to murder their officers.

$120 Extortion Charged.

Specifically, he is accused of having extorted $120 from Local 202 of the AFL International Brotherhood of Teamsters, Chauffeurs, Stablemen and Helpers while serving a term in Atlanta Penitentiary in June, 1939. He was sent there for violating federal anti-trust laws in a racket at the Fulton Fish Market.

Hustled through a police booking, Lanza was arraigned before Magistrate Frank Oliver in Felony Court. There Dewey, making his first court appearance since the Hines trial, called Socks "the boss of underworld racket domination of labor unions."

At Dewey's request, Oliver set bail at $50,000 and adjourned the hearing to Monday. By that time Dewey expects to have an indictment.

The racket boss, if convicted, faces a term up to 20 years as a first offender and a 40-year stretch if his federal conviction is considered a felony.

Held in $50,000 Bail

(NEWS foto)

Charged with extorting money from labor unions, Joseph (Socks) Lanza (right), was held in $50,000 bail in Felony Court, yesterday. L. to r., Assistant District Attorney Murray Gurfein, District Attorney Dewey, Caesar B. F. Barra, Lanza's attorney, and Lanza.

Six Detectives Guard Him.

Accompanied by members of his racket bureau and by most of the members of a current Grand Jury, Dewey walked into the crowded courtroom just before Lanza arrived with a guard of six detectives. The prosecutor made a long accusation against the prisoner, charging him with systematic extortion from several unions, terrorisation of labor executives and leadership of a mob which controlled rackets in the vegetable, fruit, cheese, fish, trucking and taxi industries.

Dewey, in asking for the high bail, pointed out than Lanza's police record goes back to 1917 and includes arrests for grand larceny, burglary, homicide, carrying a gun, extortion and conspiracy. But he never served time for a state offense.

"Why, you might as well hang a rope around this man's neck as to hold him in $50,000 bail!" protested Caesar B. F. Barra, defense counsel.

"That wouldn't be a bad idea at all," retorted Dewey.

Chapter V

The Transportation Rackets

The transportation rackets fall very conveniently into three main sub-divisions. When John New Yorker put his fare in the subway turnstile that morning he was again helping to line the pockets of a group of racketeers. This racket repeated in 1991-1993. In 1994 comes new magnetic card turnstiles as in many cities world wide.

The taxi he took from his downtown subway station over to his office represents the second major racket in public transportation one of the City's largest industries. The tractor trailer, and local trucks that delivered the supplies, and perishable shipments to the receiving department for John's two past employers represent the final group. The importance of these we have already seen.

That innocent looking subway turnstile through which so many of the City's people pass each day had long been the object of minor thefts. The Metropolitan Transit Authority, as the subway operators, had therefore found it necessary to employ a full time transit police, and detective forces of their own, in addition to the regular subway and door guards. But this did not stop the subway racketeers for an instant once their ingenious minds had conceived the plan. The plan was so simple and so lucrative when once in operation that not even the intricate checking mechanisms inside the old turnstiles, or the 1940 "new" system of hourly collection reports by bonded station agents, was able to stop it. Maintainers were employed by the City Board of Transportation to answer specific "trouble calls"[45] in their assigned stations when difficulties with the turnstile mechanisms arose. One of these maintainers named Rigney discovered quite by accident that by simply "belting" the turnstile he could turn it back any number of fares[46] he desired, but he still had no way of removing the "belted" number of fares from the turnstile without using a hacksaw or a blow-torch, which of course, would have at once given the racket away to subway detectives.

Rigney was temporarily at a loss but he soon approached a friendly station agent named Grower

---

[45]   People v Cox, Rigney, Kuch, and Carlson et al.   Record of Testimony, Par. 108-11.

[46]   Above citation, Record Folio 886-7.

and told him he would split the proceeds of a $25 to $30 "take" _daily_ if he (Grower) would give him access to the coin box and would conceal the take in his "rush hour" turnstile reports. Rigney, of course, would "belt" the mechanism for the amount of take they agreed upon for a given day. He soon had nearly all of his station agents in the racket and it wasn't long before the other maintainers and their station agents formed similar conspiracies and worked the same plan. They left out the station agents that looked honest or took care of them in other "polite" ways depending on circumstances. Cox warned other maintainers to "be careful which agents you use." Some of these agents may squeal......."[47] Some maintainers quit their lucrative jobs after several years, "because sooner or later we would wake up in Sing Sing Prison."[48] Even though they tried to bribe the Independent Subway System Court detectives that was just what happened to the whole lot when N.Y. General Sessions Court convicted them for varying terms and fines on April 26, 1940.

---

[47]   _Ibid._, Folio 889.

[48]   _Ibid.,_ Folio 900.

The subway racket seems small and a very simple case to handle, but as usual surface appearances are deceiving. True, there are no complex labor ramifications here nor "trade associations," but when we consider the number of years the racket went undetected, and the large number of men in the conspiracy, the estimated total loss to the City's subway system is simply staggering.[49]

Legally, this case on appeal[50] established a new precedent for New York State and City which should be recognized, for the success of future cases in <u>continuing</u> grand larceny and typical conspiracy racket cases. The particular Cox appeal was granted not on the grounds of guilt but on the question of whether he was legally guilty of grand larceny when he never took more than four hundred fares in any one instance. Fuld and Coleman showed on appeal that "continuous takings over a period of time, the result of a single impulse and scheme, may be charged as a continuous

---

[49] Cox <u>alone</u> stole an estimated $10,800 or some 400 fares daily per station.

[50] People <u>v</u> Harry A. Vogelstein and Abraham Cohen (Def. - Appl.), <u>Respondent's Brief</u> to New York Supreme Court, Appellate Division - First Dept., January, 1941.

grand larceny."[51] This valuable precedent is now
established for the convenient use of all rackets
prosecutors in future conspiracy-grand larceny
cases.[52] The current RICO Federal Law is founded
upon that precedent. The importance of this
precedent is that it serves as one specific
illustration to show that the Appeal Bureau and
the Rackets Bureau were carrying on the spirit of
the streamlined "Dewey indictments" and of the

---

[51]   Ibid., Respondent's Brief, p. 17.

[52]   Coleman showed me the precedents uncovered in
other states in continuing larceny cases upon
which they based this conclusion. A few of these
are:

Alabama	-	Willis v State 134 Ala. 429
California	-	People v Fleming 220 Cal. 601
Florida	-	Craig v State 95 Fla. 374
Georgia	-	Norman v state 44 Ga. App. 92
Idaho	-	State v Peters 43 Idaho 564
Illinois	-	People v Heileman 262 Ill. 322
Indiana	-	Peters v State 191 Ind. 130
Kansas	-	State v Hall III Kan. 458
Kentucky	-	Weaver v Comm. 27 Ky. L. 743
Mississippi	-	Dodson v State 130 Miss. 137
Missouri	-	State Shour 196 Mo. 202
Montana	-	State v Kurth 105 Mont. 260
Nebraska	-	Bolin v State 51 Neb. 581
Nevada	-	State v Mandich 24 Nev. 336
North Dakota	-	State v Bickford 28 Nev. 336
Ohio	-	Brown v State 18 Ohio St. 496
Oregon	-	State v Reinhart 260 Ore. 466
Pennsylvania	-	Comm. v Cook 98 Pa. Super 117
Texas	-	Cody v State 31 Tex. Or. 183
Utah	-	State v Gibson 37 Utah 330
Virginia	-	West v Comm. 125 Va. 747
Washington	-	State v Linden 171 Wash. 92
W. Virginia	-	State v Wetzel 75 W. Va. 7
England	-	Regina v Sleasdale (1848)
		2 Carr & K. 765 (larceny)

Joinder Law by removing the then evidentiary legal barriers that stood in the way of expediting criminal justice in New York County; and the U.S. RICO proves it established a lasting precedent in criminal justice, widely followed routinely today.

Undoubtedly, there will be sporadic outbreaks of the subway, and bus turnstile rackets again as long as mankind has itchy palms! Who knows if the new magnetic card turnstiles are racket proof? The District Attorneys and Federal and State prosecutors are watching and co-operating with the bus and subway detectives constantly.

Few people realize that the taxicab industry in New York represents one of the City's largest businesses. It has constantly been a source of difficulty ever since the small cab companies and larger cab fleets began to squeeze out the independent cab owner-operators. To help correct these early difficulties the City prescribed special hack laws and ordinances for licensing, gasoline and insurance, and a whole code of minor taxi police regulations enforceable by the then Police Hack Department, now the Taxi and Limousine Commission. These laws went through a gradual period of development and refinement which in itself is an interesting study. The latest two to have been added are the medallion and zoning-

passenger ordinances and earlier the horn ordinances. The New York State Legislature early recognized the magnitude of the problem the Rackets Bureau had to face here when it established the Joint Legislative Committee on the Taxi Operation, and fares in 1935. From this very Act rose one of the Rackets Bureau's principle taxi cases.[53]

The chairman of this State Legislative Committee was a respectable citizen named Edward S. Moran who simply could not resist the temptations the position opened up for him. A routine examination of the City's revenues plus a "tip" led Gurfein to look into the notoriously troublesome cab operations. Soon a thorough investigation revealed the whole set-up. Briefly, during his two years as chairman, Moran was approached by B. M. Seymour of the Terminal Cab Co., and L. Rank of the Parmelee Transportation, Co. Both were officials of large fleet taxi companies. Seymour paid Moran $500 monthly from October 1935 to March 1937, and Rank paid him $20,000. Moran simply "influenced" taxi legislation for them and obtained a one cent per gallon exemption for cab companies under an

---

[53]   People v Edward S. Moran.

amendment pursuant to the "New York State taxi bill" and the "New York State gasoline tax agreement." He also attempted to put through a bill to name Terminal and other cab companies as self-insurers in order to save them the insurance premium difference between $34.80 and $20 per month per cab. Luckily the New York Public Service Committee killed this later Moran bill.

Moran's defense was that he had received the money as legal fees, but he could make no such claim on the larger lump sums when the investigators with their usual thoroughness showed up the cautious manner in which he received the money. They also proved certain meetings such as dining car conversations after a public hearing in Albany in February 1935, or such as the March phone conversations, luncheons at the Waldorf, and $20,000 "snacks" in a restaurant. This along with the testimony of Terminal office boys such as Matthew Capiello as to the mysterious monthly envelopes, made Gurfein's case for the People air tight. Moran was convicted of political corruption under P.L. 1328 on bribes, i.e. under the Public Law on unlawful fees as a public officer. He was also convicted under P.L. 855 on extortion for graft from the taxi companies "fees." He received two and one-half years in

State's prison and was fined. Moran was then the first New York legislator to be convicted of such offenses in twenty-years. One competent authority said to me as he watched me pouring over the Moran records. "That's typical of what is going on in the New York Legislature all the time; except that this one is perhaps a bit more flagrant example of political corruption than the others."

Most of the run-of-mill taxi rackets are closely aligned with internal union violence or other types of criminal strife. One taxi case which is typical, even though it did reach rather large organized proportions (as compared to the unrelated small ingenious taxi rackets) is one in which Lorenzo Brescia, alias "Chappie," "Papa John" Andosca and Joseph Biondo were the principal defendants.[54] Following in the footsteps of the taxi racket of the notorious Arthur Flegenheimer (Dutch Schultz) and his henchman Jules Martin, these three men arranged a "protection" extortion scheme whereby they extracted from certain cab companies nearly $1,000,000 through organized gang threats. They operated the racket in the usual

---

[54]   People v Joseph Biondo, Lorenzo Brescio, John Andosco, Patsy Murray et al. (For really skillful detective work in this investigating case see Vol. II, p. 51, 7/14/39)

way, through the control of the Taxi Chauffeurs Union. Four became fugitives from justice, but the racket was nevertheless clearly broken up by the criminal investigation and the subsequent indictment, and jail terms with fines.

Although the Moran case was undoubtedly one of the most important public transportation rackets that the Bureau handled during its first year, 1938, it is far from being typical of the usual New York taxi racket cases. The usual cases involved the Transit Workers Union against the Independent Taxi Union, or company unions, license and insurance rackets, and most commonly "protection" rackets with the common terroristic coercion methods. For example, one day the police blotter showed that 20 cabs of the Allied System were struck by bottles containing acid flung from other cars. Another time 25 empty cabs were damaged when Allied systems company attempted to operate with non-union men and drivers. Often the police blotters show that upholstery was slashed, cabs set afire and drivers beaten, sometimes fatally, in the cab "protection" rackets. Frequently it is almost impossible to distinguish in these instances; whether the matter belonged to the New York State Labor Board for strikes with illegal violences by legitimate unions, for fares, wage-and-hours; or whether it is a proper criminal "shake-down" matter for the New York County Rackets Bureau jurisdiction against cab fleets and operators?

The acumen of District Attorney Gurfein then seemed to be able to spot the beginnings of an organized taxi racket without much difficulty.[55] The result was a speedy clean-up of the taxi rackets which had been so troublesome to the Rackets Bureau in 1938 and early in 1939. Ten years later we see repeats of airport passenger shakedowns of foreigners often by limousines and some by cabs. Meters with paper receipts on demand helped stop this practice. We see this however repeat again in the 1990's in an unorganized pattern.

All types of transportation, including trucking, from the heavy interstate carriers to the light half-ton pick-ups have been the "key" to the extent of racket control of many of the City's largest industries. The trucking correlation for New York City, which has already been noted for

---

[55] For instance the extortion indictment of S. Smith and J. Troue, of the Independent Taxi Union, nipped one racket in the making. Another promising baby taxi racket was caught when five T.W.U. negotiators and A. Hogan were criminally charged.

certain industries, was an invariable prosecutor's key as to whether that industry was especially susceptible to racket control or not. The taxi cab and trucking racket curve when plotted by years is one sure measure of the success of this work of the Rackets Bureau within the District Attorney's Office. Unorganized regular criminal work, of a sporadic nature of limousine, taxicab, or medallion cheating is routinely performed by the Tax and Limousine Commission, and the police. This is not to be confused with organized racketeering against honest public transportation.

For our purposes the importance of the public transportation rackets is doubly weighted, both in terms of the bus, vehicle, and trucking industry as a "control" racket; and secondly, as a time relative measure of the general success of racket prosecutions. Not only did the members of the District Attorney's Office in the 1940's realize trucking's importance, but so did the trucking racket bosses (such as Lepke and Gurrah) realize its paralytical control over the City's industrial nerve pulses. Both took definite steps towards their opposite goals.

The Dewey Special Investigation "cooperating closely with the Federal agents due to the interstate character of most trucking," invoked the then famous Federal "Big Gun Law" of 1934. Now the RICO Act of 1993, is the prosecutors best used choice against transportation racketeering. In the 1940's all acts of violence, coercion and intimidation under the old Big Gun Law were to be treated as separate offenses and carried 10 year - $1,000 fine provisions for each! Today the interstate trucking racketeers now find themselves faced with two coordinated active prosecuting agencies of government armed with new legal weapons in addition to the regular New York State Penal Law and New York City ordinances.

In the 1940's nothing daunted the various trucking "association" racketeers, the leaders of whom were Lepke and Gurrah. They dug in farther underground and tried to keep right on opening. But one by one the basic industries dependent upon racket trucking were cleaned up by the Dewey Special Investigation and later by the Rackets Bureau. We have already noted many of these trucking "association" clean-ups in the building trades, in the perishable foods, and in several of the more important groupings of the minor rackets. Others are considered in connection with their specific industries; and note the current RICO prosecutions in the following chapter. This trucking side of these main industries is by no means small or unimportant. For example, in the allied industries the trucking racket activities of "the Gorilla boys," Lepke and Gurrah added $1,500,000 <u>yearly</u> to the cost of flour alone. This then placed an extra levy upon each of the various processors before bread then reached Mrs. John New Yorker's table.

The trucking racket empire of Lepke and Gurrah reveals the main part of the City's industrial racketeering in this field. The exorbitant legends and many of their huge racket trucking "trusts" are truly as big as, and bigger than, the imagination of the detective writers can make them. The cold facts from the Court records[56] are, however, of considerable racket history value as precedents without any of these embellishments.

Almost every major <u>industrial</u> crime performed in New York City between 1931 and 1937 was purported to have been committed by these two men. All a gorilla had to say to a business man was "Lepke and Gurrah sent me," and the majority of them would quickly "play ball" or come across with the money requested. Even the New York City

---

[56]   Lepke et al, <u>op. cit., record on Appeal</u>, Vol. III, Par. 6374-6380.

Police Department labelled them "New York's number one and two industrial racketeers." At one time they assigned 46 special detectives to hunt for them and for eight contemporaries. The infamous "Little Augie" Orgen was the chief gunman on a staff of some 250 who terrorized the fur, garment, furniture, grocery, movie, night club, merchandise, laundry, gambling and legal liquor businesses, in addition to the more important ones above mentioned. The testimony further reveals that they had built up a real business supplying their gunmen and strong-arm men to employers and unions alike for industrial "troubles." For a price they didn't seem to care whether they "gunned" for capital or labor. The one fatal mistake often made in hiring them was that they often remained where "hired" and permanently put the given union, trade association, or industry under Lepke and Gurrah's control.

Through these and other means Locals 138 and Local 202 of the International Brotherhood of Teamsters fell completely under racketeer control. It is impossible, to recite all the firms and associations that were party or prey to the trucking extortion rackets of these locals, for that would approach simply copying their "records" of "business" for a period of six years and would mean very little when compiled. A conservative estimate of the Lepke and Gurrah trucking racket revenues of the late 1930's was $5,000,000.[57] Undoubtedly these two Locals combined did as well as that for themselves in a total period of six and ten years respectively of racket operation. The breaking of the trucking rackets in Local 138 began with the Dewey Special Investigation in 1935 and ended with the Goldie indictments[58] for the treacherous murder of President Snyder in 1938. Local 202 withstood the opening legal assaults of the Dewey Special Investigation although the majority of trucking racketeers did not.[59] They kept certain of its minor trucking rackets operating with uncoordinated leadership until 1939. Then Gurfein and his Rackets Bureau finished the job very completely with the Elia

---

[57] The is an average of the lowest estimates from several investigators in the District Attorney's Office and from Seidman, Thompson and Raymond, op. cit.

[58] Goldis indictments. Vol. II, p. 51, 7/2/38.

[59] For example: People v James Plumeri and John Dioguardi (under Gurfein, pleaded guilty 6/10/37)

case.[60] The independent trucking rackets outside of these limits which partially survived the Racket Bureau's legal onslaughts and later prosecutions have been those cleverly concealed. They are found in the "compulsory" handling and forced "transfer charges" at the key City collecting and distributing points, usually from interstate to local carriers. A semblance of union demands for better wages and hours hangs over those interstate racket cases. The unions now know that racketeering hurts the honest logical demands of the trucking unions for the employment of the greatest number of people consistent with higher employment against handling expediency and business efficiency. Again the twilight zone looms large.[61] But the constant vigilance of the Federal, State, and City agents, investigators, detectives, mediators, and the prosecutor's today in transportation critical points, promises that the organized super "control racket" days of Lepke and Gurrah et al, have not, and should not, recur in the 1990's.

---

[60] Op. cit., People v Nicola Elia, et al (trucking of groceries etc., by Local 202 Union drivers.)

[61] See Introduction, p. 6

We have now seen something of the three main phases of the transportation rackets and the typical cases. In each it may well be asked how do the honest men of the transportation labor unions feel about the way the Dewey Special Investigation and the Rackets Bureau cracked down year after year on some of their popular (or unpopular) elected officials. The opinion of the honest transit and truckmen working today in the much prosecuted Local 202 of the International Brotherhood of Teamsters is reflected in an editorial opinion of the then "Guardian" organ of the rank and file of Local 202. This editorial reads in part as follows:

> "...It will be remembered that when Dewey and his racketbusters first turned the spotlight on criminal activities in the labor movement, there were many union leaders and rank and filers who feared such a campaign would, to some extent, anyway, hurt the cause of labor. But it was not long before Dewey and his assistants showed that their target was not the honest union officers or the hard working honest union members, but only the parasites who live off the working men..... The labor skates who chiseled money out of the pockets of hard workingmen."

And this from the organ of the then hardest hit union of transportation workers by the Rackets Bureau. The quotation speaks for itself and for the long hours and risks then taken by the members of the Rackets Bureau for the vital City transportation rackets clean-up. Prosecutions in the 1980's and 1990's have recurred in the trucking and transportation industries, especially where interstate tractor trailers, and moving companies, as well as cash and perishables are involved. This is constantly watched by Federal, State and City prosecutors, for signs of international, interstate, and local racketeering, and early racket prosecution. With the coming increase of free trade, worldwide, public transportation racketeering must not be allowed to become a threat to all people's pockets.

Chapter VI

The Clothing Rackets[62]

Mr. John New Yorker sat at his small desk down-town in 1940 trying his best to do his small part in the company's accounts department. We can hardly believe that he was thus unknowingly working for the racketeers himself. Why? The reason is not because he was in any way dishonest or any different than the average accounts white collar desk worker. But by the very act of simply trying to move along and turn over "a little more business" billings (to use the then popular jargon) he was increasing the amount and volume of the City's industrial trade and thereby proportionately increasing the industrial racketeers' profits from business. The picture is not pleasing to say the least.

So, while John pursues his morning's tasks let us return to Mrs. John New Yorker for a moment. After getting young Johnny off to school

---

[62] The clothing rackets are discussed separately because of (1) the size of the industry, (2) the concentration of the industry and (3) the completeness of racket-control of the industry at one time and finally (4) because the clothing industry has been so greatly improved and cleaned up.

and finishing her morning house chores she decided to take a trip downtown, incidentally to look for a new jacket for little Johnny, but really to look for a new spring outfit and that light coat with a fur collar for herself.

Mrs. John New Yorker's morning shopping will conveniently serve to give us at least a framework for the most important parts of the woman's wear side of the clothing rackets.

After putting her token coin in the subway she got off at a downtown station and first visited the large clothing stores which were having their annual spring sales. To her disappointment they were all clearly above even what she could persuade John to add for the spring clothing budget. So she turned to the low priced stores on Third Avenue hoping to find something of fair quality that didn't look it's price and that would wear reasonably well. By lunch time, the sensible little Mrs. John New Yorker was still far from finding "it." Let us examine the principle cause of her difficulty, for she was not a choosey woman.

Until the latter years of the 1980's the conditions of labor in the garment and fur

industries remained distinctly submarginal.[63] The
bulk of the industry for the Northeastern half of
the United States was concentrated in an area five
blocks wide and ten blocks long, in between
downtown, and midtown Manhattan in New York City.
An ideal concentration for industrial racketeering
to prey upon both exploited labor and hungary
capital well concentrated within New York City.
Swindlers had then moved into the area and even
had offices there; all kinds of labor unions
agitated; laboring conditions were very poor; the
"stretchout," the "sweatshop," and the "yellow dog
contract" were in vogue; the professional strike-
breakers operated for the seasonal pressures, and
numerous unorganized racketeers all were "working"
this very specialized industry and area to their
own interests.[64] Such a chaotic set-up was a
hotbox under ever-increasing compression. If
Lepke and Gurrah and "company" had not stepped in
and organized the racketeering side, with the

---

[63] For pre-1930 sociological descriptions and
statistics see, Louise Odenerantz, <u>Italian Women
in New York Industry</u>.

[64] For details of this gang warfare see Thompson
and Raymond, <u>Gang Rule in New York</u>, p. 228 ff.

usual terroristic methods, in 1929, it is impossible to tell what might have happened there.

Thus some kind of "order" was brought in the late 1930's to New York City's concentrated garment industries even though it was the wrong kind. Lepke and Gurrah set up in the 1930's several clothing and fur trade associations and trucking hierarchies which they enforced with their "staff" of 250 payroll assistants. Many notorious characters met their death before the Lepke and Gurrah racket structure operated there to suit them. At one point Lepke and Gurrah asked willingly to be allowed to "vacation" a few months in the prison ward to save themselves before the Rackets Bureau and Federal agents began concurrent investigations and criminal prosecutions.

Eventually Lepke and Gurrah ran out or "rubbed out" the other gangsters and racketeers from this half-billion dollar domain.[65] For a while Lepke and Gurrah even had the City police and the District Attorney's Office rather hamstrung! And no group of clothing labor leaders or business men dared to complain to District

---

[65] For details of this gang warfare see Thompson and Raymond, <u>Gang Rule in New York</u>, p. 228 ff.

Attorneys' even when they were shaken down for as much as $50,000 annually, from the big jobbers in both the men's and women's garment manufacturing. Many of these honest frightened garment men were later very reluctant witnesses before the Special Investigation; even though the amounts they paid for "protection" over a period of years nearly broke them and forced some of them out of this very chaotic and marginal business. Honest key men in labor, business, and capital, for both the women's and men's garment industries, hesitated to tell the whole true story to the Special Investigation, or even later to the Rackets Bureau. The reason was because they knew they might have to continue to do business each month with many of these same unions, suppliers, and truckers which they would implicate.

As in 1993 profit margins in the garment industry were then very tight! Sewing jobs "stoppage" or interruption stopped their piece-worker's daily labor for bread and butter. So Lepke and Gurrah were able to operate this prize racket set-up for every cent they could force out of the half-billion dollar garment industry until 1935 when the Special Investigation first went into action.

To take a typical instance of women's dresses, the investigation showed that the Loma Dress Company had to establish two "front" subsidies called "The Leo Textile Company" and the "State Silks Co.," in order to pay the Lepke and Gurrah rackets $282,403.50 in extortions for a period of ten months only! Jimmy Hines and Al Marinelli were the political "front" for the Lepke and Gurrah racket hierarchy until they had to "look the other way." When they saw that the Dewey Special Investigation then was out to really clean up everything in the garment industries by indictments as the criminal evidence[66] warranted, the political "front" vanished overnight. Mr. Dewey was ably assisted by Mr. Gurfein (later Judge Gurfein) in this investigative and Court work at the time. When Mr. Gurfein was made head of the Rackets Bureau he took over the burden of the garment rackets clean-up task from Mr. Dewey on January 1, 1938. Mr. Gurfein returned several major indictments yearly in the clothing industries. Specific references to the dates indicated below will give the substance of these

---

[66]   See Vol. II, p. 63, .6/8 and 6/14/39.
especially p.25, 4/30/36; p.28, 10/22 and
10/27/36; and p.37, 7/10/37.

several indictments. The common factors therein revealed are: first, they all involve some elements of the crime of coercion, extortion, and conspiracy, and secondly, they represent the successive knocking out of the pegs supporting the Lepke and Gurrah racket hierarchy in the clothing and fur industries, until the top of the structure was hit with the case above cited.[67]

Then and only then, in late 1939, could any one say that the garment and fur rackets were really vitally hit the death blow by the Rackets Bureau. Order of a true non-criminal small business variety was then finally brought to the complex and concentrated garment industry in New York City.

In the $85,000,000 fur industry that was to supply the collar to Mrs. John New Yorker's new coat, the structure was an integral part of the Lepke and Gurrah racket hierarchy. Therefore the same considerations apply, except that in this fur case the "pickings" were not so choice for Lepke and Gurrah. The fur industry was not so large as the garment industry. In the second place it was not concentrated in such a small area of thirty

---

[67] Op. cit., Lepke et al, especially par. 6374-6428.

City blocks, and so readily made a racket monopoly. Shootings, stabbings, and especially stench bombings were the usual methods in the fur industry used by Lepke and Gurrah with some success. The top "association" they had for the fur industries was the "Protective Fur Dressers Association;" along with the racket control by violence and coercion of the International Fur Workers Union, the New York Furriers Joint Council, and especially of Fur Workers Locals, 1 and 2. Women workers being largely involved, the violence often was more shocking to the discredit of "silent" honest labor and honest capital.

Again there were several "twilight zone" fur cases because the industry was not so completely racket dominated as the basic clothing industries. The lower courts then in the fur rackets cases leaned over a long way on the employers' side. Later honest garment workers unions and then fur workers got real wage increases instead of lower wages from "racket" demands and extortion. Fur piece-work wages were then raised also.

The real grand clean-up in the fur industry came in 1937, when 94 defendants in the Lepke and Gurrah structure plus allied racketeers went on trial on November 7th. The Protective Fur Association, along with 44 other corporations went on trial with some forty-three men in the rackets conspiracy plus the above mentioned unions. The Federal authorities using largely the materials collected by Mr. Dewey and the Rackets Bureau did a remarkable job with their methodically timed clean-up. Many pleaded guilty, others jumped bail. Some stuck it out to the bitter end, maintaining that it had been "necessary to eliminate business competition in the fur trade for the good of the industry."[68] The fur rackets collapsed and so did Lepke and Gurrah and their mob, along with all the trucking rackets connected with it. Mr. Dewey went to Bermuda for a brief much needed rest the day this trial opened, and Mr. Gurfein and his assistants along with two grand juries reduced it to the key racket's men and followed them with indictments with many counts until most of the main Lepke and Gurrah lieutenants[69] such as the Silvermans et al were convicted and in State's prisons.

---

[68]   Reputed words of Oscar Yeager, a lieutenant of Lepke and Gurrah in the Protective Fur Dealers Association while on trial.

[69]   Op. cit., Lepke et al. Summation for defense reveals the "front" the defense tried to put up. Lepke and Gurrah were also involved in Federal charges in these industries from time to time.

With the cooperation of federal agents they caught Lepke finally; and the last of this line of cases was the indictment by the F.B.I., for murder on June 8, 1939, of "Benny the Boss" who had been an important Gurrah lieutenant in these clothing rackets. Gurrah himself had been for nineteen months a fugitive, after jumping bail. Shortly before this latter indictment he had again been apprehended by Federal agents and N. Y. County detectives, with City police cooperation.

An outstanding example of union violence was the control of Local 150, United Machinists of the Needle Industry. A conspiracy to intimidate workers and employers alike was formed. The illegal "association" extortion dues they made them pay went a long way to reaching into other interdependent garment fields for more extensive racketeering endeavors. The racketeers here were so well organized that they even had a very useful "school for sabotage" in which the best and most effective labor machine "wrecking" was practically taught. Such is the way the Lepke and Gurrah lieutenants used a control union to branch out once they had it under "racket monopoly."

Today the rackets prosecutors have only to prosecute certain small isolated clothing and fur cases that arise from time to time; and to quickly investigate any appearance of "organized" racketeering in the garment and related industries. There is still however a real social and economic problem present in the fur and garment industries as can be seen from the records of business control fights. Mr. David Dubinsky, President of the International Ladies Garment Workers Union, was then compelled to legitimately clean up the Union's act! The war threat boom caused by the U.S. Government Army Clothing orders had relieved some of the garment industry competitive pressures. It also substituted some new ones, in the return of the then notorious "speed-ups."

As long as the Rackets Bureau, the District Attorneys, and the U.S. Attorneys continue their vigilance the legitimate social-economic problem will have a chance to be satisfactorily adjusted on a competitive business basis; if the racketeering parasites are kept clear of the tempting and highly vulnerable clothing and related industries.

Chapter VII

The Gambling and Loan Shark Rackets

In the course of her mornings shopping tour Mrs. John New Yorker paused for a package of cigarettes in a small drug store. She telephoned John to meet her for luncheon and while waiting for his phone to answer watched two boys of young Johnny's age playing a slot machine. One put his quarter in the machine and watched the wheels spin around. For a moment the little ragged fellow's face shone with glee as two Bell-Fruits lined up and it looked like the jackpot was coming but (and 85 times out of 100 there was but) instead a lemon showed in the last column and he lost. He shook the machine and turned away looking rather dejected and decidedly hungry. His companion, a typical city "toughie" chided him for his loss and stepped up to another machine, a pin-ball game, and then to a Poker game machine where he fared, in the end, no better. However, he still had twenty-three cents left which was no good in the slot machines so he gave that to the drug store clerk to bet on number 233 for the next day. The latter took it as a matter of routine and gave him back his 3 cents and his policy slips, for the twenty cents on that number. The two hungry, sour-faced, kids walked out, their luncheon money gone.

Mrs. John New Yorker started to read an ad on a "firm" that would lend "easy" money on "just a signature," when John answered his phone and told the little wife he'd meet her at one of the big, downtown, popular priced restaurants for luncheon.

The incidents described above were repeated with numerous variations in persons and circumstances in many City confectionery, soda fountain, and drug stores, cigar stores, laundromats, hamburger shops, poolrooms, and club rooms, that day, today, and every day. Each and every one of the above acts represented a specific centralized racket up to the time of the beginning of the Dewey Special Investigation in 1935. There was the sales tax racket on the cigarettes.[70] There was an organized coin telephone theft racket;[71] there was a loan-shark racket, there was the slot machine[72] rackets; and there was the

---

[70] See Vol. II, p. 68, 12/5/39.

[71] Ibid., p. 21, 1/17/36.

[72] Ibid., pp. 2, 4, 6, 8, 9, 11, 20.

famous "numbers" racket.[73]   There was then no legalized gambling. The restaurant racket also was particularly vicious in the post '29 Depression years.[74]

Of these, the machine gambling, numbers gambling and the loan shark rackets were the most important and extensive, from almost every aspect, including the moral and ethical ones. They, too, were the ones that hit more people consciously, as obvious rackets.   Therefore they were the important factors that stirred public opinion in New York City to demand the Special Investigation of 1935. The other major rackets it should be remembered operated upon the regular business processes. Therefore, although they cost the City consumer considerably the major rackets are not so easily recognized by the public. However, in the three direct-cash-out rackets above, their direct impact upon the cash in the consumer's pocket could not and cannot be concealed from even the most naive City citizen.

---

[73]   Ibid., pp. 7, 34, 36, 40, 48, 50, 53, 59.

[74]   The restaurant racket is covered in detail in ch. VIII, due to its financial magnitude, wide extent, and connection with nearly every one of the other major rackets discussed.

Therefore, because of their then importance in arousing public opinion against all racketeering in the 1930's and 1940's they are isolated and specially discussed in this chapter. Legal gambling exists in numbers and racing today, but loansharking will never be legalized.

The loan shark rackets were undoubtedly one of the most socially harmful of any of the rackets. In the early 1930's the people of New York City had not fallen into the habit of installment buying from the large stores at standard rates of interest. Therefore as the Depression reached its low point in late 1932 more and more people came to the small loans men "to see them through until a break came." These men, of course, had the borrowers at their mercy and as a result rates of interest were often as high as 625% annually. When this came to the attention of Dewey he started a complex investigation of some 3,000 witnesses, willing and unwilling, indifferent or zealous. One person out of every 30 in New York City was at their mercy and Dewey himself reported that the Russell Sage Foundation estimated the then loan shark business at one million dollars weekly.

It was a big business and a big racket in every sense of the word. There were big guns, big knives, big and broken heads and no big or little jobs to be had while the small unpaid debts to the loan sharks daily grew bigger and bigger. The situation in late 1932 was simply appalling. One newspaper[75] reported just after the main loan sharking case was opened as follows:

> "Thousands of poverty-ridden clerks, taxi chauffeurs, office boys, and men and women on Home Relief hailed the investigation stroke with fervent joy. Many had suffered beatings and lived in terror after ominous threats. Shabby, broken-spirited men approached the shylock's rat holes with money scraped up at great sacrifice and pride and honor on the day of the raids and could not believe their ears when detectives met them with 'Stick your money in your pocket; your shylock's in jail.'"

In the course of his campaign for District Attorney, Mr. Dewey, who was ably assisted by Mr. Gurfein, and many of the members of the Rackets Bureau said in these loan shark cases:

> "I remember a letter carrier - a fine man - whose wife was having a baby. He borrowed fifty dollars from a loan shark because he didn't have enough money. He paid back five dollars a week for 20 weeks - a total of one hundred dollars - and then he still owed the loan shark seventy-five dollars more. I could tell you a hundred other cases just as bad."[76]

---

[75]   See <u>N.Y. Times,</u> November 3, 1935 for this particular article. Also p. 16ff, 11/1/35 et al.

[76]   Quoted in Rupert Hughes, <u>Attorney for the People</u>, pp. 75-6.

The Special Investigation's pot of 3,000 evanescent protected witnesses that had been "cooking" on the fourteenth floor of the Woolworth Building blew its lid with the thunder of a legal time bomb, when the twenty-two ringleaders of the loan sharking racket were indicted[77] in Court of Special Sessions on 252 counts. Mr. Dewey turned over all of the Manhattan loan shark cases to Mr. Gurfein and several other assistants. This time the terrified witness-victims were well protected. Twenty-two out of the twenty-two loan sharks indicted were speedily convicted and the lawyers who swarmed to their defense at first, could not then be found! A few days later fourteen more were indicted and convicted in toto. Sentences? From short stays in the county workhouse to five years in State's prison. Many of the living members of the then unborn Rackets Bureau now look back on this humane coupe with well justified pride.

Since the founding of the New York Rackets Bureau in early 1938, the work in the loan shark rackets has become less frequent for two reasons. First, the City's detectives and tax collectors

---

[77] People v Samuel Kurland, Samuel Faden, Philip Rosenthal, David Faden et al. Also, appeals affirmed July 9, 1936 and convictions upheld.

watch the so-called personal small loan firms with great care for any repetition of this situation on a wide scale. Secondly, the then Small Loans Banking Law (now New York State Banking Law) has set definite limits to the rates and kinds of interest legally allowable. This interest rate limit to date has been exceedingly well enforced. A third factor that might be mentioned is that prevailing low interest rates in the 1990's have caused more large and very reputable banking and loan houses (such as the legally regulated and inspected pawn brokers, and the well respected Provident Loan Society) to go into the small loan business, utilizing computer servicing and credit companies. This has raised the character of this devilish business into a fair, legal business activity, with legal interest rates. Thus the number and severity of the old type loan shark cases have thereby been considerably reduced. However, some loan sharking still exists in the 1990's.

The principal case in the loan shark racket of the 1930's was that of the Madison Loan Co., which had done a large small loan business; through the use of radio advertising, especially on rock and roll and on jazz programs of small stations. Seven officials of this company were indicted on April 13, 1940 for racketeering in connection with the issuance of small loans. The charge of course could this time be based on the then new bank law interest criminal violations. These men of Madison Loan Co., were convicted speedily and without difficulty. Mr. A. J. Gutreich, the District Attorney's expert accountant investigator, and his assistants were the key men in assisting the Racket Office in these loan shark cases. Their long hours of painstaking work in the analysis of account books of loan firms under investigation by the Rackets Bureau had undoubtedly been the crucial factor in the collection of evidence for many of these heartrending cases, against loan sharks to help hundreds of very poor working people.

The "Lester Plan" racket then came under loan shark scrutiny by the Rackets Bureau. Many City teachers and City employees began turning in complaints to the District Attorney's interviewers. An immediate investigation was started. Subsequently, on solid evidence, from two brothers, named Paul and Irving Unger, operating the "Lester Plan," they were indicted for loan shark "thefts" of some $50,000 illegal interest and extortions. By 1941, only one man indicted in connection with the loan shark rackets had been acquitted. Mr. Gurfein brought to my attention in these connections the fact that "even more important than the loan shark cases themselves is the publicity and the education of public opinion that comes from all these cases. That is their really important effect." For the reasons I have mentioned above, his opinion here is decidedly justified, because a shylock and his two pounds of flesh in this type of racket is often well photographed, publicized, and described in the newspapers, yellow sheets, picture tabloids and crime fiction. This aided all the Rackets Bureau's work indirectly by getting an aroused public opinion behind it.

An attempt to give a complete picture of just the gambling rackets in a county the size of New York is a study in itself. It is one which has drawn the attention of the New York State Legislature over many years. Today the various States have turned gambling revenues legally to public revenue purposes! In several States and Indian "nations" legal gambling is much in the press in 1993! Loan sharking remains illegal.

One gambling racket which had reached unbelievable proportions in New York City in the post-Depression 1930's years is discussed to give some picture of the trial methods the then prosecuting attorneys used, and continue to use, in the 1990's, in handling illegal large or small gambling rackets. The case in question[78] achieved nationwide reknown largely for other far-reaching political reasons. It shows that all phases of gambling rackets ordinarily have some ethnic, political or charity "front." With this in mind we turn at once to the notorious Hines gambling case.

Strictly speaking, the case was misnamed by the press. James J. Hines was simply a Tammany district leader in lower Manhattan who gave political and pretended judicial protection to the then illegal "numbers" or so-called "policy racket." He did the same for several other rackets; namely those of Julie Martin, the taxicab racketeer, and "Dutch" Schultz. Nice friends this district leader had! The real top men that ran the numbers racket pleaded guilty. Some disposed of each other! Many testified in behalf of the People. There were nine men originally indicted[79]

---

[78]   People v James J. Hines et al (1938 N.Y. Supreme Court)

[79]   People v James J. Hines (originally Dutch Schultz, later deceased, headed the list) J. Richard Davis, George Weinberg, Harry Schoenhaus, "Bo" Weinburg, John Cooney, Sol Girsch, Harry (continued...)

as the real numbers or policy game leaders and operators. "Dixie" Davis, the disbarred lawyer finally turned State's evidence; and with the severance of, and a separate case for, Martin Weintraub, Hines remained as the sole defendant. Therefore the main gambling racket case was in the end, People v James J. Hines. Finally, on August 17, 1938 the jury was selected and complete and the case opened. The record contains nearly a million-and-a-half words[80] for the first trial only; to say nothing of the second trial. Therefore we can only summarize briefly the substance of the case here; with especial emphasis on that part which is typical of the real technique of "busting" organized gambling rackets in New York City. These excellent methods originally developed by the Rackets Bureau have been repeated on a selected scale for all gambling racket cases. They are the usual careful, "quiet" collection of evidence, with the interviewing of hundreds of witnesses. Obtaining witnesses to

---

[79] (...continued)
Wolf, Martin Weintraub.

[80]   People v Hines, <u>Record of Trial,</u> Vols. I-V (4,600 pages.)

turn State's evidence in return for a plea bargain
is also typical. Here is a sample of the evidence
they picked on the mathematical operations of the
numbers game which visually explains its physical
operations better than many words:

Chart on No. Game[81]

Race Track Results

First Race

Stagehand	(1st)	8.20	4.60	3.40
Esquire	(2nd)		6.00	4.30
Occult	(3rd)			4.20
		Aggreg. amts. pd.		30.70

Second Race	"	"	40.60
Third Race	"	"	50.80
			122.10
Fourth Race	"	"	70.40
Fifth Race	"	"	80.60
			273.10
Sixth Race	"	"	**30.20**
Seventh Race	"	"	40.10
			343.40[82]

These men who were the bondsmen, bankers,
collectors and bookies were the key witnesses who

---

81   People v Hines, Respondent's Brief, p.7.

82   Winning No. 233, Paid 600 to 1, Odds 1000 to
1.   Also "Abadaba" after the tenth week "fixed
the 7th race and thereby the final number so
that heavily played "slips" would never win.
G. Weingbur - General Manager
Nos. Hqts. - 351 Lexon Avenue
Net Daily Take - $45,000.

were selected from several thousand by interview elimination! Three years was spent in preparing this nice little legal time bomb before even the "Numbers" higher-ups realized that the fuse was lit, or even before the press or media got wind of it. This is still typical in the 1990's of all major racket case work. This is the key to what made the work of the whole 1930's and early 1940's New York Rackets Bureau, so successful. In the 1990's decade most of the States of the U.S. have legalized the numbers gambling games to increase State Revenues and take this good revenue source away from racketeers! Federal and State income taxes are now also followed and collected on horse and dog races bets winnings in the 1990's.

A complete "lip-seal" on all out-going information was often maintained for as long as three years in the 1940's in investigating important rackets by the Rackets Bureau in order to achieve a legal blitzkrieg upon "slippery" defendants. The same trial preparation technique is widely used in the 1990's. Since 1935 there has seldom been information leaks on major cases from the prosecuting attorney's offices! There certainly never was one as long as Dewey and Gurfein were investigating the City's rackets!

There were no "leaks" in this Hines case of the 1940's to help any defendants cases.

The next step was to send in the indictments after first capturing all defendants in a county-wide net for the case. Sealed instructions were issued to the detectives conducting the raids, not to be opened until a stated hour under pain of immediate discharge and "reprisal." In the Hines case 50 raids were conducted simultaneously from Claremont Inn, in New York City near Grant's Tomb. The hundreds of "policy" gambling racketeers never knew what happened until they read in the papers the next morning that the whole group, big and small alike, were in jail. Pompez, an important numbers "banker," fled to Mexico, and Ison, became a fugitive "banker" to France. Pompez and Ison happened to be luckily outside of New York County the night the timed raid was conducted. But both were eventually arrested. Nearly all of Dewey's chief aides including many members of the Rackets Bureau assisted in this pioneering rackets trial work. They all gained excellent experience in successful investigation methods and trial techniques which has been ingeniously applied to racketeering and conspiracies ever since; especially in apprehending at the proper moment slippery rackets' defendants.

The money of Schultz (top left), the repeated votes of his gunmen like Julie Martin (top right) and of his lieutenants like George Weinberg (bottom left), helped to make William C. Dodge (bottom right) District Attorney of New York County. Schultz's vast policy racket long enjoyed immunity.

The next steps were the picking out of the known and at first unknown key defendants; and any other good key witnesses from the mob thus collected. Then came the handing down of the indictments by the Grand Jury with formal criminal charges essential therein which could be proved beyond a reasonable doubt. Many of the defendants' testimony changed and legal status also altered! Then came the careful selection of the jury, taking three or more days in itself; and finally the opening statements of the formal case itself. All these difficult processes of handling crafty and often distorted, human beings, were gone through very thoroughly to make the People's case as air-tight as possible. This occurred no matter how big or how small an organized racket existed. In this Hines case, these phases took six months!

Trial skill of the highest quality and ingenuity was displayed in this case. Thomas Dewey, Murray Gurfein, Charles Grimes, Stanley Fuld, Sol Gelb, and Mrs. Eunice Carter certainly showed their abilities, here. It was also later displayed throughout all the years of the then difficult "numbers" gambling investigations.

Murray Gurfein's ever watchful eye, had ascertained a budding taxicab racket at this same very busy time. He took to trial that taxicab racket in similar investigation style, with similar trial tactics even while the lengthy Hines trial, (mistrial, by Judge Pecora, and later retrial), and later conviction under Judge Nott went forward. Lloyd Paul Stryker, counsel for defense, certainly exhibited some skillful trial work in that case himself. The testimony clearly shows it. The Hines trial is a model case now studied often by law students, and trial practitioners, in the 1990's.

For the completeness of the picture of the Hines case methods used, here is the substance of the evidence. Hines first entered the numbers racketeering conspiracy for $1,000 per week as its "political" protector. Hines then committed himself or directed a number of acts which aided and assisted in the commissions of the crimes then contemplated. A large conspiracy was formed. First, he took part in setting up the main illegal numbers bank headquarters (Record pp. 2352-61) at 351 Lenox Ave., New York City, testimony shows. "Dutch" Schultz (shot by his own henchmen at time of trial) advised Weinburg, that the N.Y.C. headquarters were not to be opened except with

N.Y. LAW JOURNAL
Monday, April 4, 1994

CRIMINAL TERM, PART 75

Justice Fried

★ MORGENTHAU v. SALZARULO, GOLD-SMITH, BISHOP, ROTHMAN, MARTELLO, EUSTACE, NOONAN, DALY, SCARLATOS and MARTELLO—A special grand jury returned an indictment, charging the defendants—each, at one time, an elected official of the Plumbers Union Local 2 of the United Association of Journeymen and Apprentices of the Plumbing and Pipefitting Industry of the United States and Canada ("Local 2")—with the crime of Enterprise of Corruption, in violation of Penal Law §460.20 and other offenses. The indictment alleges that Local 2, which represents union plumbers performing work in Manhattan and the Bronx, has been controlled corruptly by its elected officials, including the defendants, and others, for at least the last decade.

In brief, it is charged that the defendants, and others, engaged in corrupt union activities, including: (1) extorting payoffs from plumbing contractors by engaging in and threatening to engage in acts of violence, damage to property and disruption of work; (2) taking bribes from union plumbing contractors in return for allowing violations of collective bargaining agreements; (3) taking bribes from non-union plumbing contractors in return for allowing their use of non-union workers; (4) taking bribes from contractors and individual workers in return for issuing illicit union membership cards; and (5) bribing union officials to advance the goals of the criminal enterprise.

The grand jury also directed the filing of a Special Information pursuant to Penal Law §460.30(1),[1] calling for post-conviction forfeiture of the defendants' contractual rights under Local 2's Constitution and By-Laws, including rights pertaining to the enforcement of the union's collective bargaining agreement, and Local 2 elections and internal discipline.

In order to prevent the destruction of these rights—and to prevent the further erosion of the corollary rights of Local 2 members to honest representation—pending disposition of the criminal charges and forfeiture information, the District Attorney, as claiming authority, sought provisional remedies pursuant to CPLR Article 13-A, which is incorporated into article 460 of the Penal Law.[2] Accordingly, on October 20, 1993, a Justice of this Court granted the District Attorney a temporary restraining order ("TRO") pending the determination of a motion for: (1) a preliminary injunction enjoining the defendants from exercising their rights as elected officials under Local 2's Constitution and By-Laws; and (2) an order placing those rights in the hands of a temporary receiver. A briefing schedule was set and extensive papers have been filed by all of the parties.

The defendants have moved to vacate the TRO and for an order denying the claiming authority's application for a preliminary injunction and the appointment of a temporary receiver. They argue that: (1) the contractual rights which the claiming authority seeks to forfeit, pursuant to the Special Information, are not properly the subject of provisional relief under any of the statutory provisions relied on by the claiming authority; (2) the claiming authority has failed to provide the factual bases required by Article 13-A to obtain

the provisional relief it seeks; (3) there has been no judicial determination, as required by Penal Law 460.30(2)(a), that the grand jury returning the indictment received legally sufficient evidence to establish that rights sought to be forfeited are subject to forfeiture; and (4) by appointing a temporary receiver, this court would interfere with what is described as the federal courts' exclusive jurisdiction of civil actions arising under the Employee Retirement Income Security Act of 1974, 29 USC §§1001, et seq.

Additionally, an application has been made by Local 2's parent organization, the United Association of Journeymen and Apprentices of the Plumbing and Pipefitting Industry of the United States and Canada ("UA"), for permission to intervene in this action. Included with this application is an affidavit of James R. O'Connell, counsel for the UA, which states that: "On November 10, 1993, the [UA] placed [Local 2] into trusteeship. The trusteeship, authorized under Section 92 of the [UA] Constitution, resulted in the appointment of a [temporary] Trustee who took charge of and control over the affairs of Local 2 . . . pending the selection and appointment of a permanent trustee. . . . When the trusteeship was imposed, all current officers were indefinitely suspended from office with pay. In addition, elections for Local 2 officers, scheduled for December 1993, have been indefinitely canceled. . . . The Trustee has already taken custody of all books and records in the possession of Local 2 and its suspended officers and has taken control of all Local 2 bank accounts."

On November 19, 1993,[3] I heard oral argument on these applications.

Without reaching any of the substantive arguments raised by the defendants, I have concluded, based on the unilateral action taken by the UA subsequent to the issuance of the TRO, that the TRO must be vacated and the application for a preliminary injunction and appointment of a temporary receiver denied.

It is not disputed that, pursuant to CPLR Article 13-A, a court may grant provisional relief prior to conviction. However, since "the interests of both the defendants and the government relative to the grant of a provisional remedy in a forfeiture action are weighty," Article 13-A establishes "an elaborate array of safeguards" to protect defendants from erroneous deprivation of their property through imposition of provisional remedies. Morgenthau v. Citisource, Inc., 68 NY2d 211, 221-222 (1986).

As part of these safeguards, Article 13-A requires the claiming authority to show that there is danger of the property it seeks to forfeit being dissipated during the pendency of the forfeiture action. In particular, CPLR 1312(3) provides that, "A court may grant an application for a provisional remedy when it determines that: (a) there is a substantial probability that . . . failure to enter the order may result in the property being destroyed, removed from the jurisdiction of the court, or otherwise be unavailable for forfeiture; [and] (b) the need to preserve the availability of the property through the entry of the requested order outweighs the hardship on any party against whom the order may operate[.]" In addition, CPLR 1333 provides that, "A preliminary injunction may be granted in any action under this article . . . where it appears that the defendant threatens or is about to do, or is doing or procuring or suffering to be done, an act in violation of the claiming authority's rights respecting the subject of the action, and thereby tending to render a resulting judgment ineffectual.

A temporary restraining order may be granted pending a hearing for a preliminary injunction where it appears that immediate and irreparable injury, loss or damage will result unless the defendant is restrained before the hearing can be had[.]" Finally, CPLR 1338 provides for the appointment of a temporary receiver of property which is the subject of an action pursuant to Article 13-A, "where there is danger that the property will be removed from the state, lost, materially injured, or destroyed."

In light of these standards and the actions taken by the UA, as disclosed in the O'Connell affidavit, there exists no basis for me to continue the TRO or impose the provisional remedies sought by the claiming authority. In its motion, the claiming authority seeks to prevent the defendants from exerting corrupt influence over the affairs of Local 2 during the pendency of their criminal cases by maintaining or attaining elective office and exercising the rights accorded to elected officials by Local 2's Constitution and By-Laws. By imposing a trusteeship, suspending current officers and cancelling elections, the UA has stripped the defendants of any means by which they might, now or in the foreseeable future, exercise such rights. Moreover, there is no claim that this action by the UA has been ineffective, or is in any way permitting the defendants to continue to exercise the rights sought to be forfeited. Indeed, since the defendants are barred from elective office, there is no danger of dissipation of the very rights which the claiming authority seeks to forfeit. Specifically, it does not appear that "immediate and irreparable injury, loss or damage will result" if the defendants are not restrained; nor does it appear that the defendants are threatening or are about to do, or are doing or procuring or suffering to be done, acts "in violation of the claiming authority's rights respecting the subject of the action, and thereby tending to render a resulting judgment ineffectual." See CPLR 1333. Moreover, there is no danger that the property, which is the subject of the action pursuant to Article 13-A, will be "lost, materially injured, or destroyed." See CPLR 1338. In sum, since the relief being sought, i.e., in essence, that the defendants not be permitted to exercise the rights of elected officials of Local 2, has already been obtained by the UA's imposition of a trusteeship on Local 2, there is no "need to preserve the availability of the property through the entry of the requested order[.]" See CPLR 1312(3)(b).

Accordingly, for the foregoing reasons, the defendants' motion to vacate the TRO is granted and the claiming authority's motion for a preliminary injunction and appointment of a temporary receiver is denied.[4]

---

(1) Penal Law §460.30(1) provides: "Any person convicted of enterprise corruption may be required pursuant to this section to criminally forfeit to the state: (a) any interest in, security of, claim against or property or contractual right of any kind affording a source of influence over any enterprise whose affairs he has controlled or in which he has participated in violation of subdivision one of section 460.20 of this article and for which he was convicted and the use of which interest, security, claim or right by him contributed directly and materially to the crime for which he was convicted[.]"

Hines' approval.   Secondly, Hines sought to arrange the removal of the combinations "banks" to Mt. Vernon as the New York police (Brief. pp. 15-20) were making particular efforts (then of no avail) to close the N.Y.C. "banks."   Third, Hines prevented effective prosecution in the magistrates courts by influencing two magistrates (Capshaw and Irwin) to dismiss cases (Brief, pp. 21-36) before them.   Fourth, Hines sponsored, selected and financed the campaign of the successful candidate for election to the office of the N.Y. District Attorney in 1933 named Dodge.   Dodge thereafter tried to prevent serious investigation of Hines, (<u>Brief</u>, pp. 36-40) by the District Attorney's Office into Hines own activities, and those associated with Hines, in the conspiracy.   Fifth Hines sought to prevent the appointment of Special Prosecutor Dewey because it seemed likely that such action would led to effective criminal investigation of himself, and of those associated with him in the conspiracy.   These are the real facts as revealed in the literally millions of words of the Hines trial <u>Record</u> and <u>Briefs</u>.

Picture the warm sticky courtroom with Justice Pecora presiding and Weinburg in the witness chair. On direct examination Weinburg was giving strong testimony with Hines the perfect, cool, racketeer, seated under guard in the defendants place. Weinburg is testifying, under good-looking Charley Grimes' skillful questioning, giving some very incriminating evidence on Hine's paid "political protection." All in the Court were watching and listening to Weinburg attentively. Suddenly Hines leapt to his feet. Many detectives hands felt for revolvers. The newspaper men stopped writing. The stenotype machines stopped writing. Grimes and Weinburg stopped the testimony - tension and sheer drama for a moment filled the air - Hines' face became a thundercloud and he suddenly snapped at the slouching Weinburg in the witness chair, "You lie! You know you lie!" Bedlam broke loose and when order was restored to the Court the prosecutions legal counter thrust leaped from Grimes as he clinched and unclenched his tremendous fists![83] This is a _typical_ example of what I mean by brilliant trial work on all sides.[84] None but Lloyd Paul Stryker could ever have conceived such an idea to "break" the thread of one of the prosecutors key stories. Charlie Grimes treated

---

[83] Vol. II, p. 55, 8/25/38.

[84] _Ibid._, pp. 48-70.

the unexpected onslaught for the People masterfully and quickly. The mistrial motion[85] was equally brilliant, but the People's evidence and methods won out finally. Weinburg was not intimadated, and other testimony was too clear and undisputed from the lips of the above noted principals in the notorious and then typical illegal numbers gambling racket. Hines was convicted eventually and sentenced to four to eight years in State's Prison. The proven methods of the Dewey Racket's Bureau are again needed now. In the 1990's _legalized_ gambling has kept the gambling rackets, and loan shark rackets in the 1990's at the lowest ebb ever in New York City's experience.

Let's see in 1994 if more legalized gambling in many U.S. Cities, States and Indian reservations will reopen the need to re-use these criminal trial methods against new _illegal_ gambling tax evasion and loan sharking.

Having now seen something of the typical trial methods, techniques and the main illustrative cases in the loan shark and in the gambling rackets, let us again return to the picture of that typical slot machine scene and fraudulent racket schemes so often recurring in

---

[85]   _Ibid._, p. 56, 9/11/38.

New York. This Hines trial picture best shows the difficulties faced. Police and detectives of New York City did cooperated well with the rackets prosecutors of the Hines case.

Chapter VIII

The Restaurant Rackets

While Mrs. John New Yorker walked slowly the few remaining blocks to lunch at the Brass Rail, Inc., she made up her mind then and there to question young Johnny that night to see what he and his schoolmates did with their daily milk and ice cream money for luncheon at school. Perhaps those quarter machines and gambling slips were responsible for young Johnny's latest set of pimples and for his low weight! Her maternal instincts seethed inwardly at the very thought. But before she knew it she was walking in the door of the Brass Rail Restaurant, and, spotting John at a table in the corner, she quickly joined him. The subjects of their luncheon conversation can be readily imagined!

The New Yorkers might have picked any one of some fifty of the large popular-priced downtown restaurants for their luncheon rendezvous. They still would not have avoided the racket exactions of the then notorious Metropolitan Cafeteria Owners Service Co., sometimes called the

Metropolitan Restaurant and Cafeteria Association.[86] The name makes little difference. Whatever its name it represented the top racket "trade association" of one of the worst four organized racket hierarchies [87] in New York City.

Nearly every case of restaurant racketeering handled in New York County by the Dewey Special Investigation and by the Rackets Bureau has either been directly connected with the Metropolitan or an outgrowth therefrom.[88] It is essential, then, to examine the Metropolitan case in detail as it is properly the mother of all other "baby" restaurant rackets in New York City, most of which never reached the courts for a variety of unimportant reasons, such as guilty pleas, or

---

[86] People v Harry A. Vogelstein; Abraham Cohen, Paul N. Coulcher, alias Paul Coulcher Delton; Alader Retek; Irving Epstein; Philip Grossel (Metropolitan director); Samuel Krantz; alias J. S. Kramer, alias Sammy Brown, alias Murray Klinger; Louis Beitcher, alias Louis Beecher, alias Louis Banks; William Kramer, alias Mully; Samuel Furstenburg; Charles B. Baum; John J. Williams.

[87] The other three are: (a) Numbers Racket (See Ch. VII); (b) the Lepke and Gurrah varied hierarchy (See Chs. V and VI); and (c) the Luciano prostitution-narcotics hierarchy (Ch. X).

[88] For appeal see People v Harry A. Vogelstein and Abraham Cohen, Defendants-Appellants.

because the suspects caught were on parole and therefore were returned to jail to finish their regular sentences.

A word of warning before we examine the "parent" case of <u>all</u> then City restaurant racketeering. By the latter, it is not meant to include in any way, shape, or form the use of restaurants for hideouts, frauds, "fronts," robbery or any other isolated State or Federal crimes. We are here dealing with racketeering upon restaurants within the general sense and limitations described above.[89] This warning is here repeated because one often hears a person leaving a downtown restaurant complaining of poor food or service under the blanket statement, "what a racket that restaurant is." Quite obviously this is very far from the legal meaning applied to the terms "restaurant racket." Bearing in mind this current popular semantic fallacy and recalling that every typical run-of-the mill Rackets Bureau case reviewed so far involves organized, continuous racketeering "shakedowns" let us therefore turn at once to examine the Metropolitan's structure, its methods and its

---

[89]   See Introduction, especially p. 5.

demise at the hands of the Special Investigation and of the Rackets Bureau.

Here for the first time contained within the limits of one complete lengthy case is a total and composite picture of the inner workings of a major industrial racket from its start to its demise at the date of indictment. Basically, it was a conspiracy in which extortion and attempted extortions were committed from 1932 to 1936. All of the victims were owners, managers or operators of restaurants and cafeterias in New York City and in the main comprised members of two labor unions, who were betrayed by their leaders. The conspiracy was operated by means of three agencies, apparently legitimate, but each in reality dominated and run by the above defendants and their co-conspirators. Two of these agencies comprised labor unions previously of high standards but which the racketeers had succeeded in controlling and then in operating to their own purposes. Local 16 was one of these and Local 302 the other. The former was a union of service restaurant and cafeteria employees. Besides these two unions the racketeers organized the above noted "employers trade association." This top racket association represented the principle means whereby numerous extortions over four years were carried out.

Connected with the Metropolitan were four gangsters, who in reality were the bosses of the racket. They were: Dutch Schultz; his lawyer, J. Richard (Dixie) Davis; and two other key gangsters, Jules Martin and Sam Krantz. These were the men who each received a considerable part of the restaurant racket extortion monies[90] but in actuality only the above-cited defendants were "legal" officials of the labor unions or of the Metropolitan Association. The latter men were simply the tools who did the bidding of the others and received a small slice of the payments they extorted from some fifty restaurant and cafeteria owners in greater New York!

Among the important coercion instructions employed in order to operate the restaurant racket were the well-tried schemes of forced strikes, picket lines, stench bombs, violence or threats thereof. The victimized restaurant men seeing utter business ruin and living in terror of the execution of the association's threats to them and their immediate intimates, they soon bowed to the

---

[90]   See pp. 101-105 for total amounts.

extortion demands and kept their mouths shut, for fear of future reprisals.

The methods of investigation used follow the prescribed time-bomb pattern with which we are already acquainted herein. Specifically the investigation of the restaurant situation began in August 1935 and continued until and after indictment date in October 1936. It was one of the first major inquiries undertaken by the Special Investigation and several members of the present Rackets Bureau worked in close connection with Mr. Dewey, his detectives, and accountants, upon the case. Many who were directors or somehow connected with the Metropolitan and the two racket labor unions were among those picked from the steady stream of witnesses who appeared and vanished from the inquiry office. These activities remained unknown in a large part, to the other witnesses and to the four racket bosses. A few leaks from loose-tongued witnesses inevitably, however, were bound to reach the wrong ears. The two restaurant racket lawyers, Cohen and Vogelstein, who later carried their appeals as defendants to the ultimatum, followed these leaks very closely. The record reveals they paid large sums for supposedly "inside investigation

information."[91]   Often the key witnesses who were
hand-picked to testify at the trial would not tell
the truth when brought before the grand jury, for
fear[92] of bodily harm to themselves or their
family, or of the ruination of their business.
Another fear which had to be dispelled, at that
time, was that most of the witnesses thought they
too were guilty of criminal charges simply because
they had paid the extortions demanded.   The
following oft' cited quotation from the testimony
of the defendant Engler, who had paid a $2,000
shakedown, summarizes the Special difficulties
involved in this early investigation very
concisely:

> "And whatever I lie before the Grand Juries,
> that was, I was in fear for bodily injuries
> and you know it."   (Record) 4306)

A brief review of the original indictment
resembles in form the typical Manganaro indictment
discussed above.[93]   In the Metropolitan case the
fourteen above noted individuals and the
Metropolitan Restaurant and Cafeteria Association,

---

[91]   Record, 4359-60.

[92]   Record, 2638, 2735 and 4360.

[93]   See Ch. IV, especially

were specifically named as defendants. It had then expanded to service restaurants in January 1934. The crimes as summarized above, were then in the main, conspiracy, extortion, and attempted extortion, with each defendant separately named in each and every one of the 49 streamlined indictment counts.[94] It appears from the Record, when reading between the lines of evasive answers, that the purpose of the conspiracy was obviously to extort as much money as possible without absolutely ruining the restaurants and to continue doing so by this triple-armed extortion-conspiracy plot. The 14 defendants and their co-conspirators became so efficient and so grasping that at the end of four years of operation they dominated the activities of _every_ restaurant and cafeteria labor union in New York County, besides the above noted Local 16 of the Hotel and Restaurant Employees International Alliance (racketized December, 1932) and Local 302 of the Delicatessen Countermen and Cafeteria Workers Union (racketized February, 1933). Then the Metropolitan Association decided to pile on just a little more by further sums in the guise of heavy initiation fees and weekly

---

[94]   Only the name of the victim, the date of the extortion, and the amount varies.

membership dues. Woe betide those who were threatened and didn't join!

Finally, in regard to the indictment growing out of the investigation, the last six counts deal with attempted extortions, but are otherwise similar. These deal in the main with a third labor union, Local I, a waiters union, which the defendants were _unable_ to get under their control, despite all their terroristic methods. The story of the heroic resistance of Benney Gottensman and Max Gottfried, the president of Local I, consumes many pages of praise[95] in newspapers writing about crime in New York for they bore terrific hardship and were the only really faithful and willing witnesses that assisted the investigations which saved New York's restaurant labor, capital, and

---

[95] For the human interest details and special "activities" of these "gentlemen" see Thompson and Raymond, _Gang Rule in New York_, pp. 252-268; also Rupert Hughes, _Attorney for the People_, pp. 125-190; and Harold Seidman, _Labor Czars_, pp.202-6, besides the newspaper references herewith. Thompson and Raymond over-play the "dramatics" and the small facts of human interest here. Further, they do not give an accurate whole picture. Seidman uses the "reviewers" technique of over-amplification of special facts resulting in several small inaccuracies besides his glittering generalities on money and racket methods. Hughes applies the news paper man's laudatory approach and also over emphasizes such characters as Benney Gottesman, Max Gottfried and unimportant details, such as the Metropolitan's copper plaques saying "united we stand". Good literature, but hardly real facts.

consumers much fear, hardship, and money. This is the essence and the principal burden of the structure and of the investigation activities of the gigantic restaurant racket until the time the trial opened.

At the trial, the lengthy testimony reveals that the conspiracy operated as a well-oiled whole, in which each of the defendants and their four bosses had their individual roles in true strong-arm style, "according to their abilities." These were, in part, Jules Martin and Sam Krantz as the operating directors, Louis Beitcher as the chief collector, contact man and "appeaser;" Mully Kramer as the stench bomb leader; while Coulcher, Retek, Baum and Loenig directed Local 16; and Epstein, Pincus,[96] Williams, and Borson, directed Local 302 while Grossel and Frustenburg[97] managed the Metropolitan with the advice of the two racket lawyers Vogelstein and Cohen.

The following tabulation from the testimony of the original October 1935 case[98] summarizes the

---

[96] Pincus jumped from a top story window just before trial.

[97] Pleaded guilty March, 1939.

[98] *Op. cit.,* p. 90.

better part of the Metropolitan case and appeals. It indicates the various defendants and their co-conspirators with their affiliations:

Defendants Tried[99]

Name	Affiliation
Coulcher	Official of Local 16
Retek	Official of Local 16
Epstein	Official of Local 302
Williams	Official of Local 302
Grossel	Official of Metropolitan
Cohen	) Lawyer for Metropolitan appellants
Vogelstein	) Lawyer for Metropolitan

Defendants indicted but not tried

Baum (mistrial)	Official of Local 16
Pincus (Suicide)	Official of Local 16
Furstenburg (fugitive at time of trial, but pleaded guilty)	
Kramer (fugitive at time of trial, but since pleaded guilty)	Krantz'chauffeur and stench bomb specialist
Krantz (fugitive)	

Conspirators not named as defendants

Dutch Schultz	deceased 1935
Jules Martin	deceased 1935
Harry Koenig	deceased 1936 Official of Local 16
Abe Borson	deceased 1933 Official of Local 302

---

99 Compiled from Respondents Brief, in People v Cohen and Vogelstein.

The original counts aggregated $46,290 and an additional amount of $119,500 was testified to by Beitcher as similar extortions committed pursuant to the conspiracy. Below is set forth the relevant date:

Count	Victim	Date	Amount
3	Belmont Bar Inc., and Murray's Dining Rooms,Inc.(Louis T. Brooks, President)	July to Dec. 1933	$2,300
4-7	Brass Rail, Inc.[100] (Edward Levine President)	June & July, 1934 Feb.19, 1934 Oct., 1934 Oct., 1935	5,000 500 250 300
10	Broadway Cafeteria, Inc. Isidoros Gaviris (Secretary & Treasurer)	June-Sept.1934	1,750
12	Cadillac Bar & Grill, Inc. 1460 Broadway Corp. (St.Regis Restaurant) (Max Chafkin, President)	June-Dec.1933	4,000
13	Cecil's Restaurants (Joseph Rosenblum)	August- Oct. 1933	1,500
15	Congress Restaurant (Richard Decker, owner)	Feb.6, 1935	285
22	Hollywood Restaurant (Joseph H. Moss, Treasurer)	In or about 1934, 1935 & 1936	750

---

[100] See below for special notations on Brass Rail, Inc.

23	Broadway Kosher Inn, Inc., and Four Star Restaurant, Inc. (Philip Samberf, VP & President)	March 3, 1935	500
24-28	Lindy Restaurant Corp. (Leo Linderman, Pres. & Treasurer	June 1933 Aug.-Dec. 1933 1935 Jan.-Sept. 1936	2,500 750 1,800 1,350
29	Marlboro Cafeteria, Inc. (Harry Horowitz, Secretary	Nov., 1933	5,000
30	Metropole Cafeteria (Samuel Klaye, President)	Dec.1, 1934 & Jan. 5, 1935	3,500
34	Rosoff's Restaurant (Max Rosoff, Pres.)	July, 1933 - January, 1934	3,500
35	Roth's Bar and Grill 2 places (Louis I. Brooks, Secretary)	April, 1934	2,500
36	Dairylea and Rudley Stores (Morris J. Lippman, Pres.)	October, 1934 to January 1935	5,000
37	Sagamore Cafeteria(Eli Edelman Pres.)	May 28, 1935	1,000
39	Solar Cafeteria (Charles Metzger Secretary)	May 18, 1934	255
			$46,290

In addition, there are five counts of the indictment charging attempted extortion, wherein the defendants sought to shake down their victims to the tune of $10,300.

Count	Victim	Date	Amount
43	Anne Miller's Restaurant (Anne Miller, owner)	Dec. 19,1934	$2,000
44	Brass Rail, Inc. (Edward Levine, President)	Sept., 1936	300
45	College Bar and Grill (Spiros C. Pappas, owner)	June 20, 1935	2,000
46	Gerard Cafeteria (Hyman Gross, President)	July - Dec.,1933	3,500
48	Metropole Cafeteria (Samuel Klaye, President)	July 1935	3,500
			$10,300

The names of the restaurants or cafeterias which were the victims of similar extortions but not so charged in the original indictment, together with the amounts paid, are as follows:

Restaurant or Cafeteria	Amount of Extortion	Stenographer's Minutes Record
Astor	$4,500	4514
Brighton	4,000	4514
Brown	1,000	4535
Clifford	4,000	4533
Colby	4,500	4535
Cortland	3,000	4532
Crusader	2,500	4534
Downtowner	3,000	4533
Eatomat	2,000	4539

Empire	1,500	4536
Food Mart	1,500	4535
14th Street	1,000	4535
42nd Street	7,500	4531
Grant Lunch	6,000	4540
Park Lane	3,000	4535
President	3,000	4533
Princeton & Rogers	4,000	4537,4556
Rector's	4,000	4534
Regal	2,500	4536
7th Avenue	7,000	4536
Steuben's	17,000	4654
Traffic	2,000	4515
Trinity	2,500	4538
White Way, Silver Dollar & Marine Grill	1,000	4539
Wil-low Stewart	25,000	4046
Ye-Eat Shop	2,500	4534
	$119,500	

The above tabulations indicate clearly the physical and the financial extent of the rackets, plus the absolute fascist control of labor, capital and employers necessary to exact such sums during the worst depression years from 1932-1936. We have already seen something of the original investigation of the principal defendants and co-conspirators in the original indictment, and finally something of the factual and financial structure of this unbelievable racket hierarchy.

The legal "mopping up" work of this restaurant racket clean-up inherited by the Rackets Bureau, as such, was quite considerable. For example, the important confession for trial evidence was that of Furstenburg, in March 1939, when they persuaded him to plead guilty. This was a considerable saving to the people of New York; as if the restaurant rackets had not cost us all plenty enough already. Other minor subordinates of this case were eventually also mopped up, but above all, the men in the Rackets Bureau who worked on this entire case and appeals, and similar cases since 1935, full well realize the next main job will be to catch the first signs of "repeaters" when these men are released on parole. Herein lies one of the greatest services to the people the Rackets Bureau and public prosecutors render. Recidivism by criminals often occurs, in the 1990's, again and again.

We have now clearly reviewed in some detail the techniques, methods and gradual demise of the notorious New York restaurant rackets. There remains only the necessity of a brief note upon the ultimate, original dispositions and sentences of the fourteen defendants. Four main bosses were all dead, from causes shown in the chart above, by the time of the trial in October 1936. The cause was, in at least two cases, a dose of "lead poison" from their own greedy henchmen, rather than police or investigation activities. The frequent occurrence of racketeers then killing each other and recurrence of same in the 1990's is a fact about which most newspaper and literary investigators are inclined to make much news.

Since Mr. and Mrs. John New Yorker chose the Brass Rail as their luncheon rendezvous, let us follow, for the purpose of a brief summary, the activities of it's Metropolitan and the two unions against the Brass Rail Restaurant as revealed in the testimony. The situation was one which all the restaurants above listed faced. The Brass Rail case will also show why the New Yorker's found their food and restaurant bills rising!

The Brass Rail was a pleasant popular priced restaurant located between 49th and 50th streets on 7th Avenue. Edward Levine, its president and owner, has been in the business for some twenty years, and also operated the Tavern on the Green, the famous "Sheep Fold" dining club in Central Park, and certain Jones Beach restaurant concessions. All of these became in due course prey of the racketeers. For example, in April, 1933, one defendant named Coulcher demanded of Levine, that he unionize his employees. Levine's employees were perfectly satisfied and so Levine politely rejected Coulcher's demand.[101]

---

[101] <u>Record</u> 3654,5,6.

On or about a month later, Local 16's picket line went to work on the Brass Rail. The next day, Mully Kramer threw one of his sweet "cocktails" through the Brass Rail's front door, and shortly thereafter repeated the trick down the dumb-waiter shaft of the restaurant. Martin,[102] Krantz and Beitcher, the Metropolitan operating managers, heard from Coulcher of the difficulties in "shaking down" Levine and getting his restaurants "in line." Beitcher on the witness stand, testified as follows:

> "Q. Did they tell you what to do when you went in to straighten it out?
>
> A. They did.
>
> Q. What did they tell you?
>
> A. They told me to ask for $10,000; that they would take the line off and there would be no union."[103]
>
> "Q. What did you say to Levine and what did he say to you?
>
> ******
>
> A. I told him that I was sent by the people who had gave him the picket line. I said, 'you want this picket line off; you don't want no unions; it will cost

---

102   Ibid.

103   Ibid., 4450.

you ten thousand dollars. If you don't
you are going to have plenty of trouble
and probably will be put out of
business!."[104]

Levine finally settled for five thousand
dollars in two installments of $2,500 each,[105] but
when the time came for payment Levine refused to
pay. However, after the above noted criminal
types of "persuasion" he soon paid the extortion.
Even this "settlement" however, was not permanent,
for on February 4th, 1934, Local 16 again brought
trouble upon the Brass Rail. This extortion
process repeated frequently as it did for many of
the other restaurants. And subsequent cash
shakedowns were $500 and $250 in irregular monthly
installments. This typical Brass Rail instance
happens to be one, and in fact the only one, in
which there was not united agreement of the
racketeers on the amounts and upon who should
collect it. However, until the indictment date,
Levine paid either Coulcher or Beitcher these
several sums for the "Metropolitan's "war chest"
and his own and his business "health!"

_____

104   Ibid., 4450

105   Record 3667.

-139-

In conclusion, on March 25th, 1937, the jury in the Metropolitan case returned a verdict of guilty on each and every count submitted to them except the conspiracy charges, which were suspended. The mountains of solid evidence, the excellent, selected witnesses, the timed breaking of the racket, the careful collection of exhibits, proofs, and accounts had accomplished here the same results as we have seen these methods produce in every major racket examined. The original sentence gave ten to twenty years to the key defendants discussed above and brought five to ten years upon the remaining defendants.[106] Incidentally, Coulcher received three separate consecutive sentences totaling fifteen to twenty years and stench-bombing Mully Kramer was dealt out an equal jail "vacation."

A fleeting glimpse at Mr. and Mrs. John New Yorker makes us understand then why John's check for the luncheons at the Brass Rail were a little higher that day, especially since the little Mrs. had enjoyed some of our friend Socks Lanza's sea food as a pleasant change, and John had indulged in an artichoke along with the regular vegetables, which also contributed to Ciro Terranova's large

---

[106] Record 1064.

part in the perishable foods rackets. So, with a forced smile, Mr. & Mrs. John New Yorker walked out into the street from the Brass Rail where John had, last of all, been compelled to tip a blonde hatcheek girl very generously at the racket owned concession in the restaurant.

Chapter IX

The Movie Rackets

When the New Yorkers left the Brass Rail, John went back to work to the office resolved to surprise the little Mrs. and to borrow an extra hundred dollars so she and young Johnny could have some really nice spring outfits. What the loan sharks demanded of him that afternoon in illegal interest and extortion principal money to obtain that extra hundred dollars we have already seen.[107] Mrs. John decided to give up her futile morning's clothes shopping and to take in a good movie before returning to the apartment late that afternoon.

The movie rackets are considered separately <u>not</u> because they represent, as the others do, an extensive organized racket. Curiously we are faced here with a small, highly organized, astutely operated, monopoly which over a period of years stabilized and much "improved" by non-competition the City movie business. This seemed true not only from the viewpoint of capital, but also from that of labor and management.

---

[107]   See Ch. VII.

Realization of this, based on cold figures and facts, immediately brings into clear contrast the other side of the picture, in "defense" of the racket control of a part of an industry. We are left facing the concept that reasonable control racketeering is an aid to industrial society under capitalism. This situation certainly warrants careful scrutiny and attention.

Every major racket structure examined in surveying the background and principle phases of the Rackets Bureau's work has led us step by step to the opposite conclusion. Yet the movie racket monopoly was clearly illegal,[108] both under the Federal laws and the laws of the State of New York.[109] Therefore it unmistakably fell under the jurisdiction of the Special Investigation, the District Attorney's Office and in its final phases under the jurisdiction of the Rackets Bureau. As such it has been legally and expeditiously destroyed by the usual techniques used in striking down the major organized rackets already noted. In all fairness we must ask, "Is this the exception that proves the rule or is this type of

---

[108] U.S. Constitution, Article 3, Section 8.

[109] P.L. 1926, P.L. 1433. Especially P.L. 530.

sensible 'control' racketeering ultimately of real social value as an adjunct to our industrial society?" The answer can only lie in a close scrutiny of the facts.

The movie industry of New York County is a highly competitive one. A considerable part of the movie houses are concentrated in the lower part of the City proper, and later in midtown. Being subject to seasonal and other wide fluctuations, including release contracts, employees service contracts, and cut-throat competition (with price wars!) it first fell an easy prey to the movie racketeers in 1926.

The movie racket was early scrutinized by New York District Attorney Dodge in 1931. Then the first indictment[110] was returned implicating Local 306 of the International Alliance of Theatrical Stage Employees and Moving Picture Machine Operators of the A.F. of L. The record reveals that Kaplan and Greenburg, president and secretary-treasurer, respectively, of this local took over dictatorial racket control of Local 306, suspending for all practical purposes its charter

---

[110] People v Kaplan and Greenburg et al (20 others).

and democratic by-laws.[111] Since nearly 80% of the movies in New York City were union theaters this movie operators Local 306 soon became a powerful racket weapon. The operators union Local 306 and the criminal racketeers rapidly put the movie business to their own purposes.

At this point the usual 'captive' union racket pattern seems to indicate a "blossoming out" of the racket. This was done quickly so that the operators and racketeers together could clean-up financially on the vulnerable theaters by price fixing and extortion. Thus the movie house owners that were laying the golden eggs for the racketeer union leaders, were made to prosper deliberately for the cause of greater racketeer 'dividends' or golden eggs. Let us see how.

First, theaters that were completely 'submarginal' were 'terrorized' out of business, thereby stopping cut-throat competition and admission price wars; thus stabilizing the industry at a constant high movie admissions price

---

[111] Constitution and By-Laws of the Moving Picture Machine Operator's Union of Greater New York, Local 306. International Alliance of Theatrical Stage Employees and Moving Picture Machine Operators of the United States and Canada. (especially Articles 7, 8, 9, and 10 dealing with revenues, officers and removal).2

level. Next, the racketeers forced non-conspiring high-salaried operators to be fired or union assigned elsewhere by Local 306. Third, the Kaplan Supply Co., gave the remaining movie theaters that "cooperated" with his racket monopoly cheaper equipment and supplies! Fifth, lucrative permit labor cards were issued so that all movie labor troubles and strikes were stopped. Under these conditions 'Racket' Local 306 had a $1,500,000 treasury for nearly four years. Kaplan used it as he thought best! All _employed_ movie operators had good jobs, good hours, good wages and were well satisfied. Capital was getting an 'allowed' steady small return on their investment. Movie-goers were seeing fair shows at high prices! All seemed o.k.

True enough this fair, stabilizing, movie racket monopoly temporarily proved the happy exception to the usual racket extortion pattern. It was a brief _temporary_ exception which proves the general rule, that eventually these 'honest' rackets must be wiped out of the City and kept out forever by the Rackets Bureau. Why?

Gradually the Local's racket control 'fattened' and 'softened' by the time of indictment. The non-cooperating movie operators who had become forcibly unemployed, by the Local led an internal rebellion within the Local union membership under Polin leadership, against Kaplan, and Greenburg! Independent 'theatres' with lower movie admission prices edged back into the picture. Other movie operators' 'unions' arose. One of these was a part of the Lepke and Gurrah hierarchy. It was known as the Empire Motion Picture Operators Union. Another appeared shortly thereafter called the Allied Motion Pictures Operators Union. And then Dutch Schultz tried to 'muscle in' to this racket monopoly nest also. There was movie Union Local bedlam, violence, labor union "war", and gang fights, and stench-bombings. Soon honest and dishonest men and movie-shows were suffering alike. Blood literally oozes from every page of the record in this and subsequent movie racket trials.

Kaplan, Greenburg and twenty cronies saw the handwriting on the criminal courtroom's wall. They assessed every member of Local 306, $50 for their legal defense. They wiped out their million-and-a-half treasury in a little over a year. They both went to jail after long appeals. Harry Sherman, formerly labor manager of Paramount-Publix Corp., took over Local 306 and he too had his rise and fall even before the rackets investigation could touch him and that notorious

Local 306 again. Peace and racket movie 'order' of a similar nature again came under the Lepke and Gurrah hierarchy after the original Local 306 racket had been broken. That, too, collapsed under the Dewey Special Investigation, as we have seen, and so did the Allied in good time when its turn came. So we must conclude on the basis of this case proof, that temporary, all-around, business-labor "racket stabilization" serves no permanent advantage within the industrial structures of New York City's very competitive industries.

To lean over just a little further backwards in granting temporary improvements by 'stabilizing racketeers' the following quotation is presented from the lips of a notorious racketeer:

> "As to the other 'rackets' as you call them - we call them 'business' - they're a damn sight more moral than most of the rackets that usually go by the name of corporation. Let us admit that we, the so-called racketeers, do 'extort' money from the so-called legitimate business establishments - what of it? Doesn't every other gang of business men do the same thing, one way or another? Isn't practically every thing that is sold in America sold for more than it is worth first by the manufacturer, then by the wholesaler, finally by the retailer?

> "Business is a holdup game from top to bottom. Those on top exploit those beneath them economically. Capital exploits labor - oh, and how! Big business screws small business. Of course they have made it legal and

moral. They talk of Service with a capital S and join the Rotary, both the exploiters and exploited, who, in their turn, as I've said, exploit some one below them. "Yes, we use force - what of it? Are we any worse than legitimate business? Don't big capitalists use force in putting down strikers? They stop at nothing. Of course, their force sometimes is legalized; sometimes their gunmen wear uniforms with shiny buttons on them. You told me of the 'stink bomb' gang in Brooklyn that has muscled in on a theater. Well, I can tell you for a fact (mentioning the name of a huge motion picture concern) last year, while acquiring a new string of theaters ... didn't deem it beneath their dignity to employ so-called racketeers to stink-bomb privately owned show houses all over the country, in order to buy them cheaper from desperate owners, whose customers were being driven away by stink-bombs. Or, for the matter, wouldn't you call Henry Ford a racketeer? Didn't he force his dealers all over the country, a couple of years ago, to take a certain number of cars, more than they could handle; if they didn't take them and send him the money, they lost their agencies. What do you call _that_?

"You mentioned that labor unions are hiring dynamiters and sluggers to attain their ends. Well, I may be a lowdown criminal pervert, but I don't think there's anything the matter with it. How do the capitalists treat labor? It is worse to dynamite a building than to turn out of work, in the middle of winter, thousands of men whose families live from hand to mouth? I marvel there isn't more dynamiting. If there were, I'd probably get a little respect again for the working class. Now, to hell with it! The goddam stiffs, with their docile suffering, make me sick; and if some of the gangs exploit certain labor unions, I don't care."[112]

This quotation clearly puts the case for the "stabilizing racketeer" before our eyes better than the review of any number of cases of minor movie or any other "honest" rackets. But no matter what the "human interest" side of this quotation shows, the facts from the main movie cases show that no "stabilizing" racket, in that, or in any other industry can remain permanently of any real social value; even to that particular industry at the expense of the remainder of the city's populace. We have seen from the basic legal case and following cases of the City's movie industry that they will die naturally from internal gang competitive pressures before the police and the Racket's Bureau legal pressures stop them permanently.

This question is then answered on a factual basis, for one highly competitive industry, the movie theaters. In my opinion, these same arguments apply to the other U.S. cities industries, even though the obvious evils of "stabilized" "honest" racketeering cannot be so

---

[112] Louis Adamic, <u>Dynamite</u>, p. 370. The identify of the speaker has never been revealed.

easily demonstrated for them; first, because they are not so highly competitive, and secondly, because complicated business cycle factors make the _direct_ proof for other industries far more difficult. They involve social-economic factors beyond the scope of this study.[113] Clearly no type of industrial stabilizing and racketeering, no matter how "honest," can be justified as a real aid to our City's industrial relations. Several Rackets Bureau members have agreed with me on this conclusion, citing numerous examples from their work (especially in the building industries). These "honest" stabilizing type rackets apparently brought a forced temporary prosperity for the few, at the expense of the whole people of a City. The U.S. SEC laws, tax laws, and other new laws now have attacked such "non-competition" racketeering.

To date the New York Rackets Bureau, as such, has had to handle no major organized movie theatre racket case _except_ that one connected with the Lepke and Gurrah hierarchy. It exemplifies the top movie trade Association whose collapse resulted in the ultimate clean-up of the New York City's major movie rackets. It was called the

---

[113]   See Introduction.

Empire Motion Picture Operation. It initially operated just like Local 306, except it was far more ruthless,[114] and comparatively short-lived. It never achieved the true non-competitive "monopoly" control that Local 306 did, either under Kaplan and Greenburg, or during its slow demise from further internal and external "competition" under Harry Sherman.[115]

The investigation methods used, the criminal trial techniques followed, and the regular extortion pattern was perfectly again shown as in the main Lepke and Gurrah case. It was clearly an integral part of the main Lepke and Gurrah combined case though a minor one. The beginnings of what looked like potential new organized movie rackets were disposed of by prosecuting District Attorneys in the New York City Criminal Courts as simple fraud, larceny, and extortion.

Movie theatre racketeering, like so many of the City's other formerly notorious rackets, are today negligible. This is in part due to the growth of movie _chain_ theatres as well as the

---

[114]   People v Ace Brick Corp. et al. See Ch. II.

[115]   Op. cit., Lepke et al. (Ch. VII.)

vigilance of the District Attorney's office, the Rackets Bureau, and U.S. Attorneys.

Mrs. John New Yorker would have been a rather surprised little lady if she knew that it was the same "Gorilla boys"[116] behind the raised high price of all the movies as well as behind that spring outfit! Her thoughts were instead on little Johnny and on her errant neighbor's older son as she put her token in the subway turnstile and pried her way abroad the express uptown.

---

[116] Louis (Lepke) Buchalter and Jacob (Gurrah) Sharpiro.

Chapter X

The Vice Rackets

As the wheels of the subway express carried her homeward from the movies, Mrs. John New Yorker's eye fell on a flashily dressed man seated across the aisle. He looked very much like her older son's close-mouthed haggard, mysterious friend, whom she did not like at all. He lived down the hall in their apartment building. His eyes too seemed hard, cold and shifty beneath his forcibly joyous and nervously unpleasant exterior. Perhaps because he slept most of every day and then went out for the whole night after an early dinner. Without any visible means of support, he usually had plenty of folding money. Sometimes he would borrow considerable sums from her older son, the family "black sheep," and then pay it back a few days later. She hated that type of man instinctively and quite justifiably so. Any subway detective happening along then could have told us he was a high-class "pimp," without looking twice.

The vice practices in New York have been the object of several criminal prosecuting attorneys clean-ups; Federal, State and local, of various degrees and length of effectiveness. Recidivism in vice rackets is common. We are here dealing with vice _rackets_, a very different and far less frequent illegal vicious business operation, than ordinary prostitution. Since the gay 1890's, it has become common erroneous practice to call all forms of a City's human sex vice, a racket!

Sometimes, of course, the City's District Attorney's office was called upon to prosecute "straight" vice houses racket operations chains. Mainly, to date, the office has dealt with the vice _racket_. The latter is more than simply an unorganized criminal violation of City, State and Federal laws. In contrast, the ordinary numerous run-of-the-mill unrelated vice cases seldom survive the police courts when they are occasionally caught. Many vivid descriptions of these can be found in the newspapers, in surveys, in police records and in fictional or biographical writings.[117]

---

[117] For example: _Autobiography_, Lincoln Steffins; Willemse, Lammer and Lofold, _Behind Green lights_; Richard W. Rowan, _The Pinkertons_; Louis Adamic, _Dynamite;_ Herlands, and Morelands _Commission_ Surveys, and the swarm of semi-factual fiction on the subject. By reference to the index of Vol. II of this work any specific type of criminal vice in New York City may be traced in outline for the last decade.

We are not concerned then with the bulk of these here except insofar as they have become, or lead to, some part of the Rackets Bureau's own work. It must be clearly understood that a vice racket implies a doubly <u>illegal</u> act. It is an illegal racket operating upon an already inherently illegal "business" or "service." The concept is appalling!

An excellent starting point is with the work of the Special Investigation in 1935 for there was uncovered and cracked wide open the worst of the organized vice <u>rackets</u> in New York City. Along with this went a general vice cleanup by the Police Department and the Federal agents. 1935 is also a good starting point because it represents a high point in the crime cycle and a year of vigorous and effective attack thereon. The year also represents a high point in the degree of political "protection" that vice and racketeering ever was to receive in New York City. For these reasons and because several members of the Racket Bureau were members of this Dewey Special Investigation, we begin in the year 1935 to survey the vice rackets as such.

One of the main purposes of the independent Special Investigation, instigated by New York's then Governor Lehman, with Mr. Dewey at its head, was to clear the city of organized vice. In 1935, it was flourishing openly under the political "protection" of the then, well-entrenched Tammany Mayor's political regime. Nearly all the rackets discussed in the above chapters were in full swing - or were on the crest of what proved a "hollow" victory. Then the Special Investigation caught up with them. Looking strictly to the vice <u>racket</u> field some of the more important in 1935 were: the dice table racket, the "clip joint" rackets, the gambling and numbers rackets,[118] the <u>compulsory</u> prostitution and narcotics rackets,[119] and finally, the "sucker" game ring,[120] which operated in conjunction with the latter two above. By July 1, 1936, more than 500 of these cases had been criminally prosecuted by the Special Investigation. An extra grand jury had to be called to handle the urgent case work the Racket's

---

[118]   See Ch. VII.

[119]   Lehman and LaGuardia both placed emphasis on cleaning up organized vice racketeering in these two latter fields. See Vol. II p. 7, Ref. 3/1/35 and 6/29/35; especially p.9, 10, 11, Ref. 7/2/35.

[120]   See Vol. II, p. 22, Ref. 2/1/35 for Harlem; p. 24, Ref. 4/14/35 for mid-town and p. 23, Ref. 3/21/36 for Chinatown.

Bureau was adding. By the end of August, 1936 the vice racket inquiry had reached its peak. From then on the number of vice _racket_ cases declines, right up to the 1990's.

The record reveals that the essence of the charge in People v Luciano et al[121] was that the defendants organized a scheme or conspiracy to take money from organized compulsory prostitution, and incidentally to peddle narcotics and operate "sucker games under professional hirelings" or criminal "friends." The whole set-up resembles that of the industrial case hierarchies such as that of Lepke and Gurrah except that here there were not even trade associations or anything smacking of legitimacy about the matter at all. The hierarchy was based on three units, mainly: compulsory prostitution, narcotics, and gambling. "Lucky" stood as the unknown hidden Fuhreur. Under him was his general vice staff and his own gun squad. These men in turn directed the men and women underneath them who ruled each individual in

---

[121] People v Charles (Lucky) Luciano et al (some eighteen others originally.) Mr. Gurfein and Mrs. Eunice Carter collected the original evidence which lead Mr. Dewey to start a full-time large scale secret investigation of organized narcotics and prostitution activities with such astonishing results.

the vice army. Many never knew who the "big boss" was, but each and every one of them down to the meanest, prostitute paid fixed percentages and paid heavily in mortal fear of their lives for supposed "protection" from the cops <u>or</u> from other gangs. For example, one rule was that every poor girl prostitute in a house (and 95% of all New York City "houses" belonged) paid 80% of her weekly earnings to the racket. The madam of the house got her <u>small</u> cut, the collector his, the "bookie" his, the director his, the central man his, and them "Lucky" about 40% of the original total.[122] No wonder the wretched girl making $100 per day ended up with $20 left for herself, if lucky! No pun intended. But there is little use in naming names or delving further. It is enough to know that the same type of <u>vice racket</u> worked in the gambling and narcotics end of Lucky's hierarchy just as perfectly and efficiently. This was our New York City, some years ago!

The investigation of the vice rackets went on secretly, climbing up the vice hierarchy from person to person until it was discovered from

---

[122] Luciano's income estimated as reliably as possible at $11,800,000 to $12,000,000 <u>annually</u>.

certain sources who the big boss was (*i.e.* Luciano), and gradually enough direct evidence was collected on him. Then a secret raid prepared in the inner District Attorney's circle for some five months was staged with the usual legal secrecy precision. The detectives did not even know where they were going until they got there with sealed instructions. On the night of February 2, 1935, the largest number of men and women ever held at one time in New York as "material witnesses" were clapped in jail.[123] Total bail was over one million dollars. Detectives went 80 hours without sleep, but several of "Lucky's" "general staff" big shots were caught.[124] Hundreds of witnesses were sifted, and several weeks later indictments returned. Lucky and most of the remaining "directors" were nabbed by detectives as far across the country as California. They were extradited with difficulty, later tried, convicted, and the conviction made to "stick" on appeals all the way up to the Supreme Court of the

---

[123] W.T. Jerome staged a similar "sifting round-up" in 1906.

[124] Nick Montana, Pete (Pennachio) Harris, Louis Weiner and others.

United States. In many respects the investigation, prosecution and trial methods can be seen to resemble that used in the Hines case above. Still today these investigation and trial methods are repeatedly used by the Rackets Bureau, although on a restricted basis depending on the circumstances of a given vice rackets case.

Among the men assisting Dewey in this case were several attorney-members of the Rackets Bureau and of his other bureaus within the then District Attorney's office. The core of all the cases against organized vice rackets was hit in this Luciano case when Dewey said, in the record that he:

> "...... was not in the business of prosecuting prostitutes, madams, pimps and heels. We are here to get the big shots in the vice rackets ..... we want nothing but lawful testimony."[125]

Due to skillful handling of witnesses and a deep knowledge of human psychology, direct evidence on Luciano and his vice racket hierarchy was presented for the People by Joe Bendix, Nancy Presser, Cokey Flo, Mildred Harris and Mollie Leonard. The evidence held despite the efforts of a staff of expensive, able defense lawyers.

---

[125]   Op. cit., Record, p. 149.

There we see the secret methods of investigation, timed raids and legal attacks, and then carefully substantiated indictments of the real "big shots." Astute selection of witnesses, broke the largest vice racket, along with skilled prosecution trial technique, right up to the last appeal. These were the methods that have broken and will break up any organized prostitution vice racket in the future. The same methods have been used in the 1990's against drug and gambling rackets. From its very nature, a <u>vice racket</u> with or without drugs and gambling aspects is doubly vicious and doubly illegal. Therefore all the more important it be quickly and effectively prosecuted.

<u>Vice racket</u> cases from the close of the last Lucky Luciano appeal in July, 1938, have remained for four decades at a very low level under the vigilance and cooperation of Federal agents, State law enforcement agencies; and members of the New York County District Attorney's Office, who agree with this conclusion. Since 1938, we have seen that the Rackets Bureau as such has had to deal almost entirely with the far more complex questions of industrial racketeering discussed in chapters above. Most vice rings and some vice racket vertical conspiracies have been crushed in infancy as fraud, larceny, felonies or under

P.L.2460, which is a New York State 'white slave" act. Beginning in January, 1941, there was another slow rise in the crime cycle including vice rackets. This indicates you can bet your last dollar that not a word "leaked" out until "the legal prosecution time-bomb was blown....." Vice-racket cases in the organized vice rackets starting again were stopped within a few years. Organized criminal rackets repeat themselves. You can bet they will repeat again in the 1990's. All five criminal law agencies were vigorous on the 1960's vice rackets drive and some of the old Luciano characters and witnesses were involved. There may well be new names and old names and faces in the 1990's cases. Commissioner Herlands and John H. Amen were in the 1960's doing the main recidivism prosecutions. It remains to be seen who will do the <u>vice rackets</u> prosecutions of the 1990's.

Undoubtedly, the new vice rackets pattern will follow the typical lines described above. Perhaps the new vice rackets international ring conspiracies will be quickly broken, as the gigantic international vertical Luciano vice combination was broken. Such is the <u>vice racket</u> pattern of yesterday, and perhaps again tomorrow in the 1991-1993 national U.S. recession. The

1994 continued recession in U.K., France, Europe, China, and Japan again started up the _international_ vice rackets, white slavery, and immigration rackets problems. The vice rackets with associated drugs and illegal gambling always seem to recommence in times of world economic recession.

5 Agencies Push Drive On Vice Racket Here

Hint One Jurist and Police May Be Questioned

By JAMES D. HORAN AND FRANK LEE DONOGHUE.

Copyright, 1940, New York Journal and American.

MILDRED H. BALITZER
Helped Convict Luciano

STILL OPERATING.

Herlands' probers found that the women vice witnesses who had testified at the trial of Luciano in 1937 were again operating in the '40's.

The Mayor immediately called a conference of department heads, including Police Commissioner Valentine, and ordered an immediate purge.

Several "booking agencies," where vice orders are received and filled, have already been located.

So firmly has commercialized vice again entrenched itself in mid-Manhattan that only a telephone call is necessary to book women guests for stag parties or to arrange for an evening's exotic entertainment at any one of the lavish hideaways, reports now in the hands of city officials indicate.

A sweeping investigation into organized vice, said to be flourishing on a scale almost equal to the lush days of Charles (Lucky) Luciano, was in full swing today, following orders from Mayor LaGuardia to "clean up" the town.

The probe, now under way for several weeks, was launched by the Mayor after a secret council at City Hall, where startling evidence, obtained when telephone wires in midtown were tapped, was laid on the Mayor's desk by Commissioner of Investigation Herlands.

LIMITED PROBE.

Possibility that members of the Police Department and at least one jurist might be questioned in connection with the investigation was indicated by the fact that the inquiry is proceeding along five fronts, including a drive by Special Assistant Attorney General John Harlan Amen.

Significance is given, Amen's phase of the inquiry by the fact that his investigation is limited to matters involving corruption among city officials and employes.

Another development uncovered by investigators is the use of "goon squads" to discourage free lance prostitution. As in the days when "Lucky" Luciano was vice overlord of New York, girls refusing to operate through the ring are beaten or driven out of town.

CHAS. (LUCKY) LUCIANO

ORGANIZED RING SEEN.

Investigators declare there is every indication of a well organized ring behind the new wave of prostitution, with elaborate arrangements for the furnishing of bail in cases of arrest and for court representation when the defendants come up for hearing.

So far there has been no evidence of bail bond frauds in connection with vice arrests.

Although Chief Magistrate Curran refused to answer all questions concerning the investigation, the New York Journal and American was reliably informed that Commissioner Herlands is keeping him posted on the probe with weekly reports.

Curran tacitly admitted, however, that he knew that his department was under scrutiny in connection with the vice probe, but added with emphasis:

"All I will say is that no one in my department has been implicated."

Chapter VI

Chapter VI

WHITE COLLAR CRIME AND RICO

Mr. John New Yorker had an unexpected man call on him at his office. John now worked for the New York City office of the Taxi and Limousine Commission. He had at one time worked as a cash and check receipts supervisor on parking violations tickets, and most recently for a business corporation, as a second job. The unexpected caller was a detective investigator of the Rackets Bureau. Mostly he asked John questions in the office conference room about his Commission Bureau Chief in that private conference. These questions surprised John, who soon figured out that his boss might be involved in some official bribery, or official corruption.

White collar crime involving organized crime rackets have received a great deal of publicity in the news media in the 1990's. The prosecution and conviction and sentence in 1993 of John Gotti was a most significant accomplishment for law enforcement. Like many other leaders of organized crime families, Gotti had managed to avoid conviction for his own criminal activity and the acts of his criminal rackets for numerous years despite the ongoing efforts of City, State, and Federal law enforcement agencies.

The extensive publicity wherein the Courts have ruled that the abortion clinics can use the Federal Rackets Law (RICO) to sue those who use <u>violent</u> antiabortion methods for strikes and otherwise has been now sustained by a decision of the U.S. Supreme Court. There was a nationwide conspiracy to use "organized" force against abortion clinics by bombing, threats, assults, and other violences against abortion clinics, their doctors, their patients, and their peaceful operations. First Amendment challenges to RICO use on this may well continue in the 1990's, "as a pattern of racketeering activity" had developed against abortion clinics, in a number of different locations.

There have also been a number of highly publicized white collar criminal racket cases involving prominent politicians and Wall Street individuals and firms in the securities industry. Some were vertical and some were horizontal ring conspiracies. Most notable has been the successful civil and criminal prosecution of Michael Milken and Drexel Burnham Co. in connection with securities fraud and manipulation of the high yield junk bond market. The U.S. SEC has been given renewed legal authority and enforcement methods by the U.S. Congress in the 1990's for the prosecution of securities racket conspiracies. Securities rackets are sometimes international.

The term "white collar crime" refers to a broad spectrum of legal violations committed by corporations or individuals in the course of their occupational "duties." These are often rackets. While white collar crimes are typically non-violent, their impact on their victims is often quite severe. In a recent United States Supreme Court decision, Chief Justice Rhenquist declared white-collar crime as one of the most serious problems confronting law enforcement authorities today.

White collar crime reaches beyond state boundaries and into the purview of Congress or jurisdiction of federal courts and sometimes the SEC. In order to illustrate the myriad of offenses and rackets that can be categorized as white collar crimes, this chapter discusses crimes that due to publicity and RICO are well known. Once some typical white collar crimes are recognized, the relatively new federal statutes that address these offenses are discussed. The new magnitude frequency and severity of

<u>conspiratorial</u> racketeering is this securities area of the law.

Bribery, extortion, fraud, misrepresentation, and conspiracy are strongly reappearing as <u>the</u> criminal offenses that are typical amongst white collar crimes. Bribery occurs when an individual uses wealth or influence to buy favors from a public official. The essence of bribery is the voluntary giving of something of value with the aim of inappropriately influencing the performance of an official duty. This form of racketeering by white collar conspiratorial crime is nothing new. Corrupt agreements formed where a payor finds a public official willing to sell the use of his official office have been going on for hundreds of years. Bribery is characterized as a white collar crime because the corrupt agreement is based on the illegitimate exchange of money for improper use of the authority and influence that is part and parcel of a public position. The corrupt politicians of New York City's Tammy Hall have reappeared in the 1990's rackets. Bribery is an act that allows those with wealth to buy assistance or favors that the honest citizen or common man cannot. Bribery, with racketeering, severely undermines public confidence in lawyers, in government authority and legitimacy. The lawyers professional image despite the current Reves case has suffered enough in the media!

While the essence of bribery is the voluntary agreement that produces a corrupt outcome, the essence of extortion is the use of duress to induce a corrupt result. Racketeering is both, often combined with conspiracy. Extortion involves the actual use or threatened use of coercion or duress to induce the wrongful taking of property. The extortionist may use actual force, threats of violence or exploit the inherent power of an official position in order to pressure his victim into submission. Bribery and extortion are distinct in that extortion involves a direct victim while bribery involves two guilty parties who join together in their illegal relationship.

In the context of corrupt government officials, unions and organized crime, bribery, and extortion often appear to overlap. Extortion occurs where an official or other person confronts a potential payor and demands payment because the official or other person has induced the payments through coercion. However, if the payor approaches the official or his conspirator and offers him money in return for official favors, it is ambiguous as to which crime has been committed. This situation may be bribery if the corrupt agreement is the result of a voluntary understanding between the two parties. A subtle form of extortion may really exist in a situation where an official or person in authority has a reputation for retaliating against those who fail to pay which can induce payment without any direct agreement. This scenario is common amongst corrupt politicians, organized crime families and gangs that receive "protection" money.

In today's sophisticated business environment, relatively few crimes result from the criminal conduct of a single wrongdoer. Typically, the criminal scheme that results in a white collar crime involves a group of people who have collaborated to bring about one or a series of offenses. For this reason, the prosecution of most white collar crimes involves the charge of conspiracy against the group. A conspiracy is defined as an agreement between two or more parties to achieve an unlawful objective. The essence of the crime of conspiracy is the agreement. Because the common factor amongst criminal conspirators is their agreement, a prosecutor must demonstrate the agreement or understanding that connects each defendant with the criminal activity.

In the same manner that legitimate businesses are structured to incorporate the skills of different departments, conspiracies are often formed to utilize the special skills of different groups. Just as businesses range from mom and pop shops to multinational corporations, a conspiracy can involve two people sharing a simple criminal objective or hundreds of people dividing duties amongst themselves to achieve a larger illegal goal. Organized crime involves complicated conspiracies or schemes that involve many players many of whom may not even know one another. Like manufacturers, distributors and salespeople that each contribute to the process of placing a product in the marketplace, conspirators might contribute to a sophisticated criminal scheme without having contact with all the people involved in the overall plot. Complicated conspiracies have been shown to exist in many areas of organized crime. The use of numerous groups that are connected like links in a chain pattern, or wheel pattern, to form the larger enterprise is popular method of protecting those at the top of the organized crime hierarchy. Vice rackets, securities fraud, or securities forgery, gambling, narcotics and money laundering are some examples of criminal activities that involve the crime of conspiracy. By structuring a criminal organization with many levels where each level is in contact with only the one above and the one below, the overall organization is better protected from criminal and civil prosecution if one level is exposed, and prosecuted.

A party to a conspiracy does not need to know the identity or even the number of his co-conspirators in order to be criminally liable. When an individual embarks upon a criminal venture of indefinite extent, he takes his chances as to the content and membership of the overall conspiracy as long as they are united in the common purpose as the individual understands it. The individual conspirator can only be criminally liable for the acts of the larger conspiracy if he is aware of the criminal purpose of the conspiracy and accepts this purpose and its implications. A conspirator may be liable for joining a conspiracy even if he does not agree to or know about all of the objectives of the conspiracy.

There are few, if any, criminal conspiracies in which a writing sets forth the terms of the agreement between the conspirators. A prosecutor of a criminal conspiracy will demonstrate the existence of a conspiracy by inferring the agreement between many conspirators from the conversations and acts of some of them. The prosecution does not have to prove that all the conspirators agreed on the specific details of their criminal enterprise, only that they agreed upon the essential nature of the plan. The general rule is that a particular conspirator must be shown to have had at least some general knowledge that his activity related to the broader conspiracy.

The criminal offenses of bribery, extortion and conspiracy are addressed by both state and federal statutes. These white collar crimes are most readily apparent in the context of organized crime and racketeering. In response to growing concern over the infiltration of legitimate business by organized crime, the United States Congress enacted the Racketeer Influenced and Corrupt Organizations Act (RICO) in 1970 as part of the Organized Crime Control Act. The intended purpose of RICO was to seek the eradication of organized crime in the United States by strengthening the legal tools in the evidence gathering process, by establishing new penal prohibitions, and by providing enhanced sanctions and new remedies to deal with the unlawful activities of those engaged in organized crime and racketeering. Despite the legislative intent to attack organized crime specifically, the application of RICO has expanded to include many white collar crimes.

Limitations on the powers of U.S. Congress provided for in the United States Constitution prevented Congress from restricting the implementation of RICO to individuals believed to be associated with rackets and organized crime. During the Congressional hearings prior to the enactment of RICO there was grave concern that this profound legislative attack on crime would not unfairly harass legitimate business. The movie theatre industry chapter in this book clearly shows the real differences between racket controlled unions "business," and legitimate unions work! While initially aimed at organized crime, RICO now covers a broad scope of criminal activity that includes white collar crime. Despite its name and intended aim at combatting "racketeering", the expanded application of RICO has tremendous impact on white collar criminals, not just mobsters.

RICO was intended to provide federal prosecutors with a weapon to drive organized crime out of legitimate business, but also serves to protect legitimate business from unorganized or seemingly legitimate entities. RICO expressly prohibits four activities: (1) investing income from a pattern of racketeering; (2) acquiring or maintaining an interest in an enterprise through a pattern of racketeering activity; (3) conducting the affairs of an enterprise through a pattern of racketeering activity; and (4) conspiring to commit any of these three activities.

The two key terms that are crucial to establishing a RICO offense are "racketeering activity" and "pattern of racketeering activity." The predicate offenses that constitute "racketeering activity" are numerous. These offenses include both state and federal crimes. Many of the offenses that are listed as racketeering activities have traditionally been viewed as white collar crimes.

"Racketeering activity" includes, to name just a few: bribery, extortion, counterfeiting, embezzlement, obstruction of justice or law enforcement, interference with commerce, gambling, money laundering, tampering with labor organizations or unions, and numerous forms of fraud, especially mail fraud, wire fraud, securities fraud, and banking fraud. A "pattern of racketeering activity" exists where there are two or more acts of racketeering activity committed within a ten year period.

The prosecution of a RICO case requires proof of five elements. The prosecution must show (1) the existence of an enterprise which (2) affected commerce, that (3) the defendant committed two or more predicate acts (4) which constituted a pattern of racketeering activity, and that (5) the defendant invested, maintained an interest in or participated in the enterprise.

An enterprise can be any individual, partnership, corporation, association, or group of individuals that are either a legal entity or associated in fact although not a legal entity. This flexible definition has encompassed groups such as a terrorist group, a motorcycle gang, a police department, unions, a senator's office, a prosecutor's office, and law or accounting firms. Honest lawyers and honest accountants are now protected (somewhat by the current U.S. Supreme Court Reves case) from RICO liability, where they provide professional services but do not participate in management. The enterprise can be either a legitimate business as we see in movie theatres or trucking or an organization set up for the purpose of committing crime. In white collar cases, the enterprise is almost always a legitimate business which serves as the instrument through which the criminal defendant(s) operated illegally.

The impact of the enterprise on commerce is what provides prosecutors with jurisdiction to bring a RICO action in federal court. The Commerce Clause of the United States Constitution provides the federal government with jurisdiction over interstate and foreign commerce, and consequently the authority to invoke the RICO provisions. Use of the federal mail system, acquisition of a foreign corporation with proceeds of criminal activities, interstate shipment of goods, interstate communications by phone are all examples of activities by an enterprise that affect commerce.

The most common criminal offenses that occur in white collar prosecutions under RICO are wire fraud, mail fraud, securities fraud, bribery and embezzlement. Two or more offenses committed within ten years are required to establish a pattern of racketeering activity. These two or more acts must somehow be interrelated and indicate some form of continuity. In order to prove a pattern of racketeering activity the prosecution must show that predicate offenses are related and that they amount to or pose a threat of continued criminal activity. The courts have developed in the 1990's both the continuity and relatedness requirements in order to restrict the expanding application of RICO to long term criminal conduct.

The substantive RICO offenses are the investment of racketeering proceeds in an enterprise, acquiring or maintaining an interest in an enterprise, and participating in the conduct of the enterprise through a pattern of racketeering activity. There must be a connection between the predicate acts and the affairs of the enterprise. In the context of white collar crime, proof of this connection can be difficult to demonstrate because the enterprise is often a legitimate business that is the passive vehicle for the illegal acts of others. While the predicate acts must have some connection to the enterprise, these acts do not have to benefit the enterprise. The significant factor is the position of the defendant within the enterprise which enables the defendant to commit the criminal acts.

The most significant advantage of RICO for prosecutors is that it allows for the prosecution of multiple defendants in one proceeding. RICO allows the prosecution to portray the entire extent of crimes committed by an enterprise.

Rather than attacking the leader of an organized crime family or a small number of subordinates for a single crime, the prosecution can present its case against the entire hierarchy of the organized crime family for the diverse criminal activities in which that enterprise engaged. Instead of proving in Court one criminal act in a defendant's life, RICO allows for the presentation of a defendant's entire life of crime or all the illegal activities of an organization. Thus, RICO reaches behind the apparent crime scene to expose both the white collar worker, or professional (who can be a part of an organization that is involved in criminal activities), and businesses that conduct their affairs through systematic or institutionalized criminal conduct.

The benefits of RICO are well illustrated by the 1984 prosecution of the entire upper echelon of the Colombo crime family. Fourteen defendants were identified including three bosses, five captains responsible for supervising and protecting the criminal activities of the family and six lower ranking associates of the organization. In this case the prosecution established the existence of an ongoing criminal enterprise by demonstrating that the organized crime family selected an acting boss to direct its activities while the boss was serving in jail! Traditional conspiracy law of the 1920's would not have allowed the prosecution to unite all these defendants in a single proceeding or to identify the specific roles of each of these defendants within the enterprise. Additionally, RICO's requirement of proving a pattern of racketeering activity allowed the prosecution in the Colombo case to join in a single proceeding the widely diverse state and federal crimes that the Colombo family had engaged in for over a dozen years. The Colombo indictment included charges of extortion, drug trafficking, gambling, loansharking, and both state and federal bribery offenses. Because participation in a racketeering enterprise is a continuing offense, RICO allowed the prosecution in the Colombo case to include crimes that were committed in New York, New Jersey and Florida.

State and federal law continues to combat white collar and organized crime. The application of the Racketeer Influenced and Corrupt Organizations Act to white collar and organized crime has provided prosecutors with a means of directly confronting criminal activity that previously may have escaped prosecution. The criminal offenses of bribery and extortion are now both individual crimes and the predicate acts for establishing RICO violations which now allow entire crime organizations to be prosecuted. Both legislators and law enforcement agencies and District Attorneys continue to adapt and expand the old successful Rackets Bureau investigation and trial techniques, and utilize the legal process to address the growing sophistication with and without computers of white collar and organized crime. Such criminal activity will be increasingly punished and deterred. The Federal Racketeer Influenced Corrupt Organizations Act (RICO) has aided State and City Rackets Bureau work substantially since its enactment in 1970.

Also Intra-State racketeering patterns that were seen in New York in the 1930's and 1940's have recurred again in the 1980's and 1990's; often now with sophisticated white collar legitimate "front" coverup businesses as a shield. Businesses, both legal and illegal, go interstate and international, so rapidly today, that RICO is essential to effective U.S. rackets prosecution.

In the 1990's one of the biggest and rapidly growing industries will be <u>legal</u> gambling. It is a large industry with some $325 Billion gross intake, netting well over ten (10%) for most entrepreneurs thereof. There are new Indian Casinos, new riverboat gambling, new racetracks, and new numbers lotteries.   It widely effects restaurants, hotels, the eaters, nightclubs, and even sports arenas, and public amusement parks, etc. States realize millions in taxes from gambling and betting which will decline with vastly increased legalized gambling and legal betting.   In 1994 only Utah and Hawaii have not legalized certain types of gambling under State and local control.   Gambling on the Mississippi River boats and on many Indian Reservations has become the latest legal gambling hot spots as States are so eager for new revenue sources without new taxes.   Can illegal rackets be kept out in the 1990's? We will soon see. It will be a real challenge to tax collectors and prosecutors to keep racketeering out of this vastly expanding newly legalized industry, even with the help of RICO and new State laws and enforcement!

Chapter XII

COMPUTER CRIME

Mr. John New Yorker in 1939 did not have a computer on his desk, but only a hand operated adding machine and a one-hand telephone. Now in the 1980's and 1990's, advancements in telecommunications and computer technology have enhanced business efficiency and productivity throughout U.S. and international society. The computer age has created methods of communication and processes for exchanging information that were inconceivable not all that long ago. Technological innovation allows tasks that were once performed manually or mechanically in hours or days to be done electronically in seconds. The development of smaller and more powerful computers in conjunction with sophisticated telecommunication network satellites, and fiberoptics now has transformed the local work place into a global arena. Laptop Computers today have more capacity, memory, and communications, than rooms full of large 1970 computers!

Unfortunately, the extraordinary developments in computer technology have also provided the means for crime through the use of modems and computers. As computers continue to enhance the pace of our information driven society, the ability to commit crimes quickly increased. The advances of computer technology have created new opportunities for abuse and crime which the legal system has struggled to address. Deliberate computer crimes arise from the vulnerability of government and corporate computer systems to deliberate intruders, and hackers.

Computers influence our lives everyday in countless ways and are unavoidable in our modern society. From birth till death our lives are recorded, monitored and controlled by computers. Almost every white collar worker utilizes a computer or computer generated information in their daily duties. Every worker realizes that computers allow employers, the government and the business community to readily access information that not long ago seemed private, personal or confidential. While the advantages of computer technology are tremendous, so is the potential for its abuse. The computer has provided the opportunity and the means for the increasing commission of crimes such as illegal access, theft, fraud, grand larceny, and invasion of privacy.

Those who work with computers, and develop an expertise in their use, must be deterred from applying their skills to the vices of criminal activity. Before the computer was invented, the amount of property that an individual could steal or destroy was limited by cunning, and the physical ability of the wrongdoer. Throughout history the extent of larceny has been largely dictated by the ability of the robber to transport his loot. Crime has been revolutionized by the computer. Today, through the use of modern technology, criminals can access financial records and transfer large sums of money without the immediate threat of physical detection! Recent criminal law has upheld the confiscation of electronically transmitted money laundered funds through bank and financial institutions channels and computers.

The gravity of the threat posed by computer crime cannot be underestimated. A recent survey conducted by the American Bar Association reported that fifty percent of businesses and agencies questioned were victims of financial and other computer crime. Twenty five percent had suffered losses between $2 million and $10 million a year. The most frequently reported crimes involved the unauthorized use of computers for personal purposes, the use of computers to steal corporate assets, the destruction of computer stored information, theft of computer software, embezzlement and fraud against consumers, investors and institutions. Computer crime is often a serious 1990's racket.

Despite heightened efforts by law enforcement agencies and professional organizations to evaluate how much computer crime occurs and determine who commits it, there is a great deal of uncertainty in the statistics. The extent and frequency of the commission of crime through the use of computers is difficult to determine. The number of computer crimes detected is uncertain, and the percentage of those detected and subsequently reported is unknown. Many computer crime victims believe their best interests are served by not reporting the commission of computer crime. Corporations _fear_ embarrassment and the negative publicity that could damage their sales and financial reputations if the extent of their computer crime losses were reported. Many remember the past racketeering fears which are now on an international and interstate computer business basis. Furthermore, confusion exists because there is no universally accepted definition of "computer crime."

There is agreement, however, that the potential for computer crime is great, probably now greater than any other type of crime. The computer is no longer the exclusive instrument of highly trained scientists or statistics crazed bureaucrats. Local, state, federal and city governments use computers. Businesses rely on technology to compete in the corporate jungle. The world's financial markets would be crippled without the instantaneous exchange of computer information. The number of computers in use has multiplied exponentially due to the introduction of the personal computer in homes and everywhere. The small powerful computer has been developed, marketed and presented to our society which is eager to take advantage of its many uses.

Some early abusers of computer technology appear to be more clever than dangerous. Now computers have become racketeers tool's also. In the early 1980's, the news media gave great attention to computer "hackers" who were able to access large computer systems with the mere use of modem telephone links and simple laptop computers. The stories about the ease with which these "hackers" were able to "play" their sophisticated computer "games" created great concern that legal action was needed to be taken to prevent these unwanted criminal intrusions. Connected by modem through the telephone system to the data banks of multinational corporations, these "hackers" demonstrated that computer crime was a reality that had to be addressed by the Federal, State and City legal systems. While some "hackers" were merely exploring their technological curiosity causing little or no harm to anyone, the power of the small computer made any unwanted intrusion a grave threat. Misuse of a computer can cause great damage, and even if damage does not materialize, the potential consequences of intentional misuse could not be easily dismissed. The development of the computer virus and its notoriety in the 1990's provided strong evidence of the severity of potential destruction that can be easily introduced into unguarded computer systems. Many today are cleverly guarded.

Michelangelo is known around the world for his profound artistic achievements. Thousands of tourists and art lovers alike travel to the Italy each year to view the ceiling of the Sistine chapel and stand in awe of his magnificent marble sculpture of David. However, the name "Michelangelo" was given to a computer virus that threatened to disrupt business and government computer systems nationwide in March of 1992. A computer science student at Cornell University created the virus and released it with the intent to have the virus spread nationwide through computer software to computers systems. A computer virus attacks computer systems without warning through the exchange of contaminated software. The extent to which a computer virus is able to spread is limited by the ability of computer operators to anticipate the particular type of program that spreads the virus like "Michelangelo" and design protective software to avoid the destructive results of the virus. Fortunately, the Michelangelo virus was early detected and proper precautions were taken by most computer users to protect their systems from the destruction of this ill intended "Michelangelo." However, this virus, and many others of similar design, destroyed hundreds of thousands of dollars of software, and computer property. What might seem to be clever or imaginative to one with such highly developed computer skills can wreak havoc and cause enormous loss through the intended or even unintended criminal misuse of computer technology.

Because computers can be used for destructive as well as constructive purposes, State and Federal lawmakers have been compelled to enact legislation in order to deter the misuse of computer technology and protect the property and privacy of society. In 1970 Florida enacted the first computer crime legislation. Other states soon responded to the recognized threat of computer fraud and misuse. Today, forty eight states and the Federal Government have computer trespass statutes that establish the foundation for prosecuting computer criminals. The acts that constitute computer crimes are all common law crimes that the states had long recognized. The unique twist of computer crime is that its perpetrators use computers to accomplish their goals. All the States had criminal statutes that prohibited the types of conduct engaged in by computer criminals; but many States responded to the demands of computer facilitated crime by enacting legislation that addressed the particular nature of these acts.

The statutory penal law of New York in the 1990's establishes five computer offenses. The crimes of unauthorized use of a computer and computer trespass are both aimed at the unauthorized use of a computer or computer service. The offense of unauthorized use of a computer is committed when someone without authorization knowingly uses a computer which has a device or coding system designed to prevent such unauthorized use. The requirement that the

computer have a protection device to prevent
unauthorized use was intended to encourage
businesses and the computer industry to implement
safeguards against computer crime. The crime of
computer trespass does not require the violated
computer system to have a protective device. It
only requires the intruder to access computer
information (such as computer programs business
trade secrets and private or classified government
data) with the intent to commit a further felony.
Racketeering and criminal conspiracy are sometimes
found in the investigation.

New York also criminalizes computer tampering
which is the destruction or alteration of a
computer program or data. This offense expands
the crimes of larceny, forgery, false written
instruments and related offenses to include such
conduct as it relates to computers. New York's
penal law prohibits both the unlawful duplication
of computer related material and the possession of
computer related material. The theft of a
computer program or data through unauthorized
duplication is unique to the electronic medium.
Unlike traditional larceny or theft of material
property, computer programs and stored data can be
taken quickly through duplication without
disrupting the owner's actual possession of the

property or depriving the owner of the program or information. It is significant that both the act of duplication and the possession of the information are separate criminal offenses. Someone who receives a duplicated program or data is held criminally liable as well as the actual thief.

In addition to state law prohibiting computer crimes, the Federal government has enacted legislation in order to protect its own computers and address computer crimes that reach beyond State boundaries.

In 1984, despite fear of Federal overreaching and redundancy with state legislation, the United States Congress enacted the Computer Fraud and Abuse Act. The 1984 Act addressed three specific areas of criminal computer abuse. <u>First</u>, access to a computer without authorization in order to obtain classified government defense, foreign relations or nuclear information with the intent to harm the United States or benefit a foreign country was made a felony. This was done in the interest of national security. <u>Second</u>, the Act declared unauthorized access to a computer in order to gain information from a financial institution or consumer reporting agency to be a misdemeanor. The purpose of this section was to deter "hackers" from accessing computerized financial information from institutions that were federally insured. Privacy protection was another premise underlying this prohibition. The mere observation of such computer data is sufficient to establish a criminal act, removal of the information is not required. The third prohibition made the unauthorized use, modification, destruction, or disclosure of information from a computer operated by the United States a misdemeanor. Here the concern was to protect the computers of the Federal government from outside intrusion.

The 1984 Act was extremely narrow and failed to address a number of serious computer crime targets. While State law was to regulate the crimes of trespass, malicious mischief and theft that occurred within each state, interstate computer crime needed to be Federal regulated. Since the activities of corporations and financial institutions reached across state boundaries a means of prosecuting computer criminals and racketeers was needed as their intrusions often reached beyond State and national boundaries.

Accordingly, Congress amended the Computer Fraud and Abuse Act in 1986 to clarify the language of the Act and add three new areas of

protection.   The Amended 1986 Act created a
federal computer <u>fraud offense which is somewhat</u>
<u>analogous to the federal mail and wire fraud</u>
<u>statutes</u>.   Congress extended the protection of
computerized financial and credit records to all
parties transacting with financial institutions
including   individuals,   partnerships   and
corporations.   Finally, in response to the spread
of computer access codes by illegitimate computer
operators, the 1986 Act prohibited the trafficking
of computer passwords. This was intended to deter
"hackers" from sharing or trading passwords or
other confidential data through pirate bulletin
boards.   Trafficking   in   illegally   obtained
computer information that affects interstate or
foreign commerce was the basis of this offense.

Both State and Federal law criminalizes and
regulates certain computer oriented activity. The
federal   legislation   addresses   matters   of
compelling federal interest and federal criminal
acts that state and local officials are not
capable of controlling. Federal law enforcement
resources are better equipped to investigate and
prosecute areas of computer crime than state and
local authorities. In enacting the Computer Fraud
and Abuse Act, Congress did not want to discourage
both State and Federal prosecutors from joining

their efforts to eradicate computer crime. The States have their own interests to protect. They are well suited to locally handle crimes committed within their borders. However, most racket computer crime is interstate.

Whether at the state or federal level, computer crime must be deterred. Computer crime victims should be encouraged to both report incidents of unauthorized computer access and implement effective means of deterring computer crime through their own increased security efforts. Most computer crime is committed by University or employee insiders; not by juvenile "hackers" operating from telephone booths or their rooms. These "insiders" should be locally monitored and educated in the proper use of technology. Because the use of computers in the 1990's has proliferated in our society in such a short time, many computer users have failed to appreciate the long standing values of privacy and property with regard to their own use of computers. The computer can pave the way to greater prosperity and efficiency; or can become the instrument that undermines our traditional values. Both police and detectives, as well as racketeers in the 1990's use computers.

Unfortunately, the choice between constructive and destructive computer crime applications remains to be determined by the adequacy of the law, and the prosecutors, to address jointly the rapid evolution of this criminal technology. International money laundering is currently the foremost racket example. In computer crime, under RICO as well as computer crime laws, there may be <u>both</u> civil and criminal penalties for deliberate computer criminal activities. Where corporations and conspiracy is involved, of several persons, then both civil and criminal penalties will apply, especially where securities and monies are involved with computers.

Chapter XIII

FORGERIES AND FAKES

Mr. & Mrs. John New Yorker had enjoyed their Dali prints but had recently seen for sale other "original" Dali prints in several stores. They worried much about their Dali's authenticity and decided to consult an expert about it, whose name their lawyer gave them.

"I'm truly sorry to give you bad news," Mr. Charles Hamilton said to Mr. & Mrs. John New Yorker who came to consult with him at his office. "Your signed Salvador Dali prints are nothing but cheap, pirated copies. And the signatures of Dali on them are just clever forgeries." "But we have certificates of authenticity from the art dealer," protested Mr. John New Yorker. John produced a fistful of sucker-dazzlers certificates from the portfolio under his arm.

Each warranty was beautifully printed, ornately bordered so that it looked like a stock certificate, and each was adorned with a flashy gold seal from which fluttered a multicolored ribbon. "The man who gave us these certificates told us he was a personal friend of Dali and that Dali had signed the prints in his presence. He gave us a printed folder which tells all about the rarity of the prints. On top of this, he gave us his personal guarantee that the prints would double in value within a year."

Mrs. John New Yorker asked: "Are you absolutely certain that they're fakes?" Mr. Charles Hamilton, one of the nation's top graphologists assured her they were. She began to cry, and said: "We drew out all our money from the bank, every penny of it, and invested it in these prints so that when they doubled in value, we could sell them and make a down-payment on a home. Is there any way we can get our money back?"

"You can try," Mr. Hamilton said. "I'll help you in any way I can. But this art dealer you bought them from is no longer in New York. He never stays anywhere more than a few months." "His method of operations is simple. He rents a fancy store front with a big plate glass window that bears some impressive name, such as 'Galerie Internationale de Paris.' Then the dealer proceeds to glut that city with bogus art work. That dealer sold thousands of the forgeries to other dealers on New York City's Madison Avenue; all at 'bargain prices.' The dealer-seller touts his fakes as 'great investments' and produces a folder with laudatory comments from satisfied customers (all non-existent) who have allegedly made a fortune on Dali prints. If you walk into his gallery, he tells you anecdotes about his 'old friend Salvador Dali,' and then sells you for $800 dollars a print worth no more than $2. Later, as the complaints start to come in from swindled customers, the dealer packs up his wares and vanishes. He soon reopens under another fancy name in another city while the police and the F.B.I. play hopscotch trying to catch up with him."

"Take a walk down New York City's Madison Avenue and you'll see his bogus wares in many of the windows of art dealers. Or read the catalogs of some of the smaller art dealers. Go to the auction house in your neighborhood and you'll find that signed Dalis are being knocked down at ridiculously low prices--a sure tip--off that the auctioneer knows they're fakes."

Dali is not the only modern artist targeted by the deft-fingered gentry. A friend of mine visited Paris several years ago and strolled into an art gallery on the Left Bank. The walls were covered with signed prints, but the gallery appeared to be empty. However, there was a partly open door leading into the rear of the gallery, so my friend took the liberty of seeking out the owner. In the back room he discovered, hunched over a large table heaped high with Picasso prints, a gentleman with a pencil hard at work lettering something on the bottom of one of the prints. He peeked over the man's shoulder and was astonished to see that he was signing Picasso's name. Sensing my friend's presence, the man turned with an apologetic grin and said in French: "Don't worry. These are for the American market only. We export all our personalized prints to New York where the Americans appreciate our Parisian touch!"

During the past two decades, millions of dollars worth of faked Picasso, Miro and Dali prints, many of them also "manufactured" in New York City, have flooded the market.

Equally overwhelming is the number of bogus Chagalls. If Marc Chagall had signed all the prints that bear his counterfeit signature, he would have been the first artist in history to die from writer's cramp!

Mr. Charles Hamilton a well-known graphologist and forensic documents examiner (handwriting expert), was recently called upon to testify in a case involving the sale of more than 300 forged Chagalls to a Japanese art dealer in New York. Half way through the trial, with the jury nodding assent to his testimony, the defendant (possibly the forger of Chagalls) offered to settle the case. He agreed to remove all the faked signatures from the prints and present them to the dealer, plus pay $50,000 in damages.

Because of the plethora of forged Chagall signatures on the New York market--they proliferate at the smaller auctions--he prepared for art buffs a short statement explaining how to identify the forgeries;

Marc Chagall (genuine signature)

Marc Chagall (forgery)

Salvador Dali (genuine signature)

Salvador Dali (forgery)

How to Identify Marc Chagall's Authentic
Signature:

1. The second peak of the capital _M_ is lower
    than the first.

2. The base of the center curve of the _M_ is on a
    level with, or nearly on a level with, the _a_
    that follows.

3. The _arc_ of _Marc_ is always written on the same
    level, one letter with another, and level
    with the base of the center curved stroke of
    the capital _M._

4. The _c_ in _Marc_ is always separated, and formed
    separately, from the _r_. Never joined to the
    _r_.

5. The capital _C_ is _Chagall_ tends to be
    upright, not markedly leaning forward.

6.   The second small _a_ in <u>Chagall</u> usually (but
      not always) has a peak that sticks up on the
      second vertical stroke.

      As a handwriting expert, Mr. Charles Hamilton
is called upon several hundred times every year to
give an opinion on suspect documents--wills,
I.O.U.'s, anonymous letters, contracts and other
financial instruments. Police and prosecutors are
forever amazed at the huge number of amateur
racketeers in New York City who fancy they have
the ability to swindle an expert with their
amateur creations. They do not realize that the
expert, long trained in all the tricks of fakery,
can often spot a forgery ten feet away. When a
handwriting expert examines a document, the last
thing he looks at is the shape of the letters in a
questioned document. He is always initially much
more interested in comparing the disputed
signature with a genuine signature to study the
slant, size, pen pressure, speed of writing, and,
above all, the relationship of each letter to the
adjoining letters. The expert knows that it is
relatively easy to copy the exact shape of
letters, and some forgers have been successful at
this. But to capture the precise appearance of a
document or signature, with every letter in its

proper place in relation to adjoining letters, is a task that mocks the most adroit counterfeiters.

There are forgers who, right now, are fabricating wills to defraud their relatives, or knocking off literary and historical autographs to gullible collectors. It takes a sharp eye to catch them all, but a trained expert, like Charles Hamilton who may have examined two or three million documents during his graphology career, can usually spot a forgery without much difficulty and pinpoint its defects. Some counterfeiters make a specialty of Abraham Lincoln documents. The profits from the Lincoln forgery racket alone amount to millions of dollars every year. The victims are usually wealthy collectors who fail to check their purchases with the same cunning and care that they exercise in making their other investments.

Nearly all the large brokerage houses now and then invest a client's money in junk bonds without first obtaining a discretionary release. When the client discovers that his money has vanished in a brokerage or "bucket" shop, and was invested without his permission, the brokerage house may require the services of a forger (often the broker himself) to create a release bearing the customer's "signature." Thus a criminal racket conspiracy often begins. It then becomes Mr. Hamilton's job, or the job of some other forensic document examiner, to identify the authorizing discretionary release to the brokerage house as a forgery. Forgery conspiracy of this type proliferate after every major market "crash." If you believe you have been victimized by your broker, or by a broker conspiracy consult an attorney and, if he thinks you have a case, he will first seek out a handwriting expert and then help you to recover all your losses. Forgery rackets don't survive arbitration or the Courts.

The relic racket is also an old one that challenges the skill of amateur racketeers and cheats. Some years ago, when Mr. Hamilton was in the relic business, he was offered what purported to be "the skull of Adolf Hitler." The skull was accompanied by a sheaf of affidavits and authentications that proclaimed it genuine. It even has a bullet hold in the right side of the head (Hitler was alleged to have shot himself, as well as biting into a cyanide tablet). Mr. Hamilton compared the skull with an official X-Ray of Hitler's head taken soon after he was injured in an unsuccessful attempt to kill him on July 20, 1944. In the fake, the teeth were much too perfect to be Hitler's, whose mouth was "a dental disaster." Nevertheless, Mr. Hamilton was amused enough to pay $150 for the skull; and a reporter from the New York Times found the skull interesting enough to write a story about it! For a while the skull grinned sardonically from a table in Mr. Hamilton's living room, much to the horror and dismay of his visitors. He finally sold it to a collector of unusual fakes for precisely the amount it had cost him!

Even more unusual than Hitler's faked skull was the Cardiff Giant, dug up in New York State in 1869. A farmer who was digging a well uncovered a huge nine-foot high figure of what appeared to be a petrified man. The behemoth weighed a ton and a half. The farmer and his wife put the figure in a tent, hired an old Indian to tell stories about how his ancestors had warred against giants, and sold admission tickets to a gullible public. Many university professors swallowed the tale and the cagey P.T. Barnum, whose museum was then on 14th Street in New York City, paid $37,000 for the stone man. Eventually Professor Marsh of Yale tested a tiny piece of the Cardiff Giant and found it was made of plaster of Paris!

Forged relics are regularly sold unknowingly for racketeers by many of the auction houses in New York City. Sometimes the fakes are "spotted" before they are sold and sometimes not. For example in 1991, Sotheby's catalogued for sale a two-page letter of George Washington dated from Philadelphia, September 12, 1796. The estimate of its value was $10,000 to $15,000. Mr. Hamilton examined a copy of it and found that the letter was a forgery. The owner was forced to withdraw it from the sale, and sold it to Mr. Hamilton for $35.00; and it now forms a part of his personal collection of fakes.

Just a few years ago, Sotheby's auctioned off for $10,000 a tall silk hat that supposedly belonged to Lincoln. It was not Lincoln's size, but no matter. The late Malcolm Forbes, my classmate bought it for display in his collection. To this fake, he added the "binoculars that Lincoln used in Ford's theatre on the night he was murdered." The binoculars were allegedly found on the floor of Lincoln's box the day after the murder, according to an affidavit that accompanied them. Since Lincoln's box was only nine feet from the stage, and Lincoln was six feet two inches tall, he likely would have bumped actress Laura Keene on the head if he had held the binoculars to his eyes and leaned out of his box to get a better look at her. Despite the questionable provenance, Malcolm Forbes shelled out $25,000 for them!

Make a fool's tour of New York City any day and you'll find dozens of forged relics for sale, from Queen Anne's chamberpot to Jesse James's six-shooter. Every relic has a sheaf of affidavits and I-swear-to-Gods that proclaim its authenticity! Even the most vigilant police force or most alert of district attorneys have not halted the proliferation of such fakes, in the 1990's.

An old acquaintance of Mr. Hamilton's paid for his forgery crimes by three years in prison and is now leading an honest life. He is an expert on American furniture and possesses awesome knowledge. He and Mr. Hamilton toured an exhibit of rare American furniture to be sold in New York City, at a large auction house. "See that piece over there," he said, pointing to a chest of drawers. "It's advertised as American, but it's British." "How can you tell?" "The wood, for one thing. The design for another. Then there's the craftsmanship. I'd bet a dollar that it's got a Philadelphia cabinet maker's label pasted on the bottom. A forged one, of course. It did. "And take a look at that three-legged chair!" I looked where he pointed and saw a chair with four legs. "Ph," said his acquaintance, to Mr. Hamilton smiling, "perhaps I should explain. It has three genuine legs and one peg leg." A glance in my catalog proclaimed the chair to be all original. "Sure it says that. But the left rear leg is a Philadelphia style original." "What's Philadelphia-style?" "Well, when a dishonest furniture dealer wants to replace an 18th century chair or table leg, he merely has a craftsman carve an identical leg of the identical wood that's in the rest of the chair. Then he buries the new leg in manure for a year. It gives the leg a patina. After a brisk application of matching polish for the whole chair, including the peg leg, only an expert can spot the replacement."

Charles Hamilton's acquaintance is also an expert on American silver and even wrote a book on the subject that now sells for about three hundred dollars. He made a die punch from a genuine Paul Revere silver marking, then with a quick blow of a hammer added Revere's hall mark to old previously unmarked pieces of American silver, such as bowls and teapots. He sold a number of these fakes to the Dupont Winterthur Museum before the experts there put a magnifying glass to the Revere markings and found that the old silver, not being malleable, had received microscopic fracture marks on the impact of the fresh strike.

There are other "craftsmen" at work making articles in silver and gold with forged hallmarks. You must be constantly on guard against them. New York is filled with counterfeit Egyptian statuary, faked Aztec and Mayan vases and figurines, and bogus Russian icons. Make sure you are buying from a reputable dealer, and don't buy any "rarities" until you have got a second opinion on them. Although sellers of fakes risk a prison sentence, the risk is not great. These racket culprits often merely plead innocence; pay a small fine; and are released on parole from crowded prisons to continue selling their forgeries. Witness the so-called "genuine" Rolex watches, street peddlers are selling on the Avenues of New York City!

Twelve years ago Mr. Hamilton wrote a little article on Christie's and Phillips, two famous British auction houses which have imported a superior air from the old country. As the British peddle a full quota of forgeries, I'll give you Mr. Hamilton's impression of their attitude and operation, as it was published more than a decade ago in LEADERS MAGAZINE, Vol. 4, 1982.

I've watched for several years a known racket with a sort of grim amusement and without comment. Philips, Son and Neale sold certain bogus or misdescribed historical letters and documents. Late in March 1981 Charles Hamilton visited Phillips with another friend, James Kramer, to glance over the pre-sale exhibition of some books and autographs in which he was interested. He noticed in Jim's catalog the description of a letter of Sir Walter Scott, dated 1830, about some illustrations for Waverly.

"This is an amusing item," Hamilton said to Kramer, "because I know it's fake even before I look at it. I've seen it and have examined it before." Mr. Hamilton asked one of the pleasant two young ladies in the room to bring him the folder containing the "original" letter. James watched with curiosity as Hamilton took the letter out of the auction folder. "Notice," Hamilton said, "that is a pretty good copy, accurate in most details and with a postmarked address." But, Mr. Hamilton added, handing the letter to Kramer, "just lift it up to the light and read the watermark." Mr. Kramer raised the letter and looked at the water mark. It was dated 1832, two years after Scott wrote the letter! "You see," Hamilton said, "it was at best, inadvertence, that caused Phillips to catalog this fake as genuine. Certainly the cataloger could have put this letter up to the light and read the watermark date."

Today Christie's and Sotheby's hawk anything with or without catalogue caveats that brings a sale. In 1992, Christie's offered a baseball jersey worn by Lou Gehrig, estimating its value at $400,000. However, it was withdrawn, not because it was smelly and in need of washing, but because it lacked the "right" label. Sotheby's has gone Christie's one better and is proudly peddling old comic books in the same sumptuous sales rooms that once enticed wealthy Japanese (now long gone from the auction arena) who paid astronomical prices for fashionable art.

Not long ago, an elderly gentleman showed up in Mr. Hamilton's office with a painting of a Munich church that was signed "Adolf Hitler." Hamilton looked at the painting and found it was not in Hitler's style and bore a fraudulent signature. "Sorry," Hamilton said to the owner. "This is a forgery." The old man took the news calmly and Hamilton asked: "Where did you get it?"

"From a curiosity dealer in Brooklyn."

"Well." "you should take it back to him and exchange it for some other curiosity."

"There's a bit of a problem," said Hamilton's visitor.

"I'd already bought a Sioux warbonnet from him, and it turned out to be a modern fake. I exchanged the warbonnet for this painting."

"Give it a third try," Hamilton said.

"Well, about two years ago he sold me a very rare early New York map, in color, dating from the time of the Revolutionary War. He guaranteed it, but when it turned out to be a forgery, he took it back and gave me the warbonnet in exchange."

At this news, Hamilton burst out laughing, and said: "Go back to him once more and tell him: "This time I don't want a fake, I want something genuine!"

A few years ago the mania for collecting movie stars was so rampant that eager collectors paid huge prices for signed photos of the celluloid legends--Marilyn Monroe, Humphrey Bogart, Clark Gable, Rudolph Valentino--the list of desirable names grew and grew. And whatever is collected is always fair game for individual forgers, or forgery racketeers. There were fifty faked signatures of Marilyn for every one that was genuine. A good forgery of Marilyn that could fool anybody but an expert fetched $2,000 and inexperienced collectors never paused to consider the question of authenticity, but battled for the privilege of acquiring those same fakes. Today collectors are more discriminating and hard times have descended on the racket forgers of movie stars.

But there is no sanity in Mudville: The collecting world is now in the grip of the wildest and most irrational craze of all time. It is a racket so fierce and uncontrolled that it makes the tulipomania pale by comparison. Hamilton alludes, of course, to the collecting of baseball memorabilia. Baseball card forgeries are fairly easy to identify. The paper is too thick or too thin, the printing is often fuzzy, the photographs lack crisp clarity and the wrong typeface is often used on the verso of the card. Since many cards sell for hundreds, even thousands of dollars, it's worth the collector's effort to learn the earmarks of the fakes.

Mr. Hamilton as a handwriting expert, is in the eye of the holographic hurricane. Almost daily he is consulted by collectors and dealers who wait with suspended breath for his decision-- real or forged? When a mere signature of Shoeless Joe Jackson--not a signed baseball or glove, mind you, but just a signature from an album--fetches $27,000 at auction, (far more than the average handwritten letter of Washington, Lincoln or

Napoleon), it is time to study the rampant racket forgeries in this strange hobby!

The old days when the amiable Babe Ruth and equally amiable Lou Gehrig gave away their signatures to kids are long gone. Heroes of the diamond now sell their autographs for top prices. They sign plaques, photographs, baseballs, gloves, and mits under contract, and these manufactured products, warranted by certificate to be genuine, are hawked on television and in department stores. Baseball signatures are big business and fetch millions of dollars every year. Result: a proliferation of racket forgeries that already swells beyond the number of authentic signatures. Companies are organized just to peddle forged plaques and signed photographs. This conspiracy and racket has blossomed. Prosecutors and honest business both moved against these forgery racketeers. Only a few months ago Mr. Hamilton was retained by a large legal firm to stop the machinations of a big business devoted to selling fake baseball items. Of course, it was claimed they did not know they were fakes!

Consider the astronomical prices fetched by baseball memorabilia. A 1951 Topps Mickey Mantle rookie card in flawless state brings $40,000 or more; a uniform of Roger Maris sold for $131,000 in March, 1992. The tops for some years of all baseball cards, was an 80-year-old Honus Wagner card which fetched $451,000 in 1990. These prices have in the 1990's brought a plethora of racket fakes onto the market. Remember the 1927 Flo-Joy ice cream cards picturing Babe Ruth, which forgeries soon far outnumbered the genuine article. Racket history repeats itself.

In the morning's mail (October 14, 1992) Mr. Charles Hamilton received a handsome circular from Macy's that proclaims "Owning a piece of sports history is a phone call away"! and adds that you can buy a plaque or baseball signed by Mickey Mantle for only $99.00. Others available on baseballs (at only $49.00) are Reggie Jackson and Hank Aaron, and if you are willing to up the ante $10.00, Tom Seaver and Willie Mays. You may, I think, safely assume that Macy's has carefully checked the authenticity of the signatures they are selling (Joe DiMaggio was offered $1 million to sign 9,000 baseballs and 56 bats. He declined the offer.)

To combat the exploding number of forgeries, Robert Abrams, the Attorney General of the State of New York, proposed, legislation to regulate vendors of signed baseball items and protect purchasers from forgeries. Their proposal included a certificate of authenticity with every item sold for $50 or more.

As fast as one phony racket business in fakes and forgeries is suppressed, others spring up. In the 1990's they sell their products by mail, by radio, by television, and over the counter in variety stores and wherever souvenir items are offered. There are, of course, many ethical companies who actually have baseball players under contract, and who offer products bearing authentic signatures. The problem for the collector is to weed out the racketeers. Most forged sales are by organized rackets.

There are no set rules or set procedures in catching forgers. As the New York District Attorney knows, forgery is a felony. Some forgers work alone and are not rackets. It is an elusive felony. Most forgers are in racket conspiracies and are like eels who slip through the police net at the last moment. Today forgery is often difficult to detect. It infiltrates our lives from every angle and exists in almost every profession. Remember that rare coins and stamps, as well as relics and paintings, are often forged. The best advice is to keep alert at all times and deal cautiously with all persons you don't know.

Chapter XIII

Conclusion[126]

When Mrs. John New Yorker stepped off the subway for her racket rented apartment[127] she walked out of the racket "fixed" subway turnstile,[128] and bought a new magazine at the racket owned news stand,[129] stopping on the way at a "controlled" grocery store,[130] unhappy over her futile day's clothes shopping.[131] So she picked up some spaghetti and meat balls,[132] for supper, along with Larry Fay's "controlled" milk, and Manganaro's "priced" fruit for dessert. Next she

---

[126] Appendix B for complete case listing of the Rackets Bureau's work since 1938, by years.

[127] Vol. II, pp. 58 and 59. Also Ch. V.

[128] Chap. III.

[129] Chap. II.

[130] Chap. IV.

[131] Chap. VI.

[132] Chap. IV. Ciro Terranova;s foods specialty were these particular foods supporting the $1,450,000 racket "Union Sciliciano."

set out homeward to fix up this supper for her two John's.

Young Johnny got home from school around five and Mommy wasn't long in finding out that his luncheon quarters had gone in the Costello and in the Shapiro brothers slot machines[133] instead of for the cafeteria[134] next to school. Mr. John's arrival home with the loanshark[135] hundred dollars for her new spring (Lepke and Gurrah) wardrobe[136] didn't cheer her up much. At supper she forced herself to talk of the (Kaplan "controlled") movie[137] of that afternoon. The forged baseball photo was on the living room table. After supper Mr. John read his racket newsstand evening paper[138] while she helped young Johnny into an exorbitant racket installment purchased bed.[139] A few hours later after an evening night-cap of

---

[133] Chap. VII. Also Vol. II, pp. 2-11.

[134] Chap. VIII. Also Vol. II, pp. 19-65.

[135] Chap. VII.

[136] Chap. VI.

[137] Chap. IX.

[138] Chap. III.

[139] Vol. II, p. 24, 4/4/36.

racket diluted whiskey Mr. and Mrs. John New Yorker decided it was bed time. Then a quick shower,[140] and Mr. John New Yorker turned out the racket manufactured light switch.[141] Soon he was joined by the little Mrs. in her racket made pajamas. Even their dreams were troubled by the thought of the money the family black sheep son owed the pimp in the neighboring apartment.[142] Small wonder they couldn't understand why all City prices were getting higher. So ends the story of a couple of months in the life of the average middle class New Yorker family of 1930's post-depression years.

The above were ordinary necessities of everyday life on which the New Yorkers then paid higher prices, due to criminal racketeering. Why they had to pay exorbitant prices just to enjoy the normal necessities of life has been reviewed in the preceding chapters, with the most illustrative and typical case for each major "industry."

The basis of "type" racket case selection herein was in each instance checked with the

---

140   Chap. II; also Vol. II, p.24, 4/14/36.

141   Lepke and Gurrah, Ch. VII.

142   Chap. X; also Vol. II, p. 22ff.

District Attorney's Office or with a member of the New York Rackets or Appeals Bureau who had handled that type of racketeering, either originally or on appeal. Often ten to twenty cases had to be reviewed for each chapter before any such "type" case could be definitely established. Frankly, in others the selection was clear from the beginning as in the clothing, restaurant, gambling and vice rackets. This case method of survey clearly has brought into evidence definite patterns for all organized City racket prosecutions. Let us pause to review what this consistent, tried and successful prosecution pattern reveals itself to be.

There is first the matter of investigation of a "suspected" racket, "using" either labor, industry or capital as its starting racket. Investigations are always conducted secretly. For example one detective recently shot himself from pangs of conscience over a vital information leak and bribe. Next, the grand juries indict the defendants. The prosecutors subpoena the necessary witnesses. The press often cooperates and is occasionally deliberately misled by authorities to publicize other racket news far removed from an intended big clean-up of a different racket hierarchy. Investigations may run for one day to as long as four years if necessary. Conclusive factual evidence is prepared and no word on the real investigation is revealed until the real big "hidden" racket bosses are ascertained and the timed raids are simultaneously conducted. Next, material witnesses are carefully sifted, and usually some turn state's evidence, due to sentence recommendation promises and skillful criminal psychology. Any fleeing defendants are carefully and persistently traced until returned to face indictment. Appeals are sometime prepared for higher courts <u>before</u> the original trial even opens. Certain "Ace in the Hole" evidence may be withheld subject to rules of evidence and disclosure until needed at a crucial trial. The trial itself is made as brief[143] and as effective as possible. Excellent criminal trial psychology is often clearly demonstrated in the large number of guilty pleas, and in handling of clemency and sentence recommendations. In the 1990's sentencing guidelines are in effect for the Courts, and under much criticism.

---

[143] For example: streamline indictments, Joinder Law and consistently excellent brief court Summations by the People's young attorneys prosecutors.

Of course, the trial preparation pattern is usually much abbreviated to fit the given circumstances of any particular racket case. Occasionally it is altered so as not to duplicate any Federal rackets work. We have already seen several of these exceptions to the general pattern especially in connection with the trucking rackets. But the general investigation patterns for successful legal racket trial prosecution demonstrated in each one of the main City rackets described herein remains the same in subsequent prosecutions.

Many lawyers predicted in the 1940's that the New York County Rackets Bureau would not have the force and vigor that the Special Investigation demonstrated in prosecuting against both the rich racketeers and the poor racketeers of New York City. They felt that the cloak of legal unionism which the remaining racketeers had adopted, plus the pull and haul of political and financial pressures might lead the Rackets Bureau to become simply a mediocre, ineffective investigating aftermath of the Special Investigation. Such has been far from the case as the various prosecution records of the 1980's and 1990's clearly demonstrates.

In the 1990's, District Attorneys, Federal, and State prosecutors have well learned how the Dewey "time bomb" general investigation pattern worked in the inspired 1930's and 1940's anti-racketeering drive. With expanded laws they have also put renewed vigor into their work. With RICO they have again attacked white collar crime, computer crime, forgery, labor racketeering, and other rackets, (especially involving political connections), just as strongly as the original Dewey late 1930's investigations had done!

Although the most flagrant of the racketeering hierarchies in New York City's industries had been dealt a staggering punch by the 1930's and 1940's Special Investigation, the much later New York and Federal prosecutions spared no efforts in following this up. They picked up numerous new leads to millions of dollars of racketeering in other City industries. The New York City District Attorneys with Federal cooperation immediately set out in the 1990's recession the especially mean recurring rackets against the poor. These are now repeating and very similar to those "busted rackets" in the Dewey Special Investigation of 1935.

The 1930's Dewey racketeering investigations showed the successful methods that led to indictments against government officials. For example, the pattern cases in the 1930's included a former State Commissioner of Motor Vehicles, Charles A. Harnett and a State Assemblyman named Edward S. Moran, Jr. An unusual investigation of an isolated racket was the 1930's case of Judge Martin T. Manton. The racket case against Judge Manton, formerly Senior Judge of The United States Circuit Court of Appeals for the Second Circuit, was turned over to the Judiciary Committee of the U.S. House of Representatives, as a basis for possible impeachment proceedings. The Federal authorities made much use of New York Rackets Bureau process in indicting Judge Manton before a Federal Grand Jury. Manton immediately resigned from the bench, and was subsequently convicted. The successful patterns of New York County Rackets Bureau official investigations is still being used by Federal prosecutors today. The F.B.I. used that same "time bomb" investigation pattern in the unusual criminal non-rackets case of Sol Wachtler in 1992! A pattern "time bomb" case of the 1930's against racketeering public officials, like Moran, the Chairman of the Joint Legislative Committee on Taxicab Fares, was used to obtain that officials conviction. He was sentenced to 2 1/2 to 5 years in State's Prison, for bribery in the taxicab racket. Another "time bomb" case that of Charles A. Harnett's was stopped at trial, as Harnett went into a mental hospital.

The 1930's Rackets Bureau also began wide spread investigations into political corruption in the letting of contracts by the State and City! These political cases have recurred in every decade. Conducted secretly, as usual, it was not made public until after the year, 1939, when William Solomon, a political district leader, and Charles Mullins, Assistant State Comptroller, were indicted for bribery and convicted the following year. History repeats itself in the types of rackets recurring against the public and also in the proven successful methods to stop them. These are now reinforced by the RICO Act and new laws in the 1990's to fit the new computer crimes and white collar crimes, etc.

Another pattern of "time bomb" investigation involving labor union fronts occurred in 1939 in a lucrative racket in the trucking of retail fruits and vegetables. It was caught by the Rackets Bureau in the so-called "1204 case." The defendants were officials of the Retail Fruit and Grocery Clerks Union, Local 1204, and were indicted for conspiracy and extortion being subsequently convicted for the latter. Other important indictments were obtained in the union labor field of perishable foods when several officials of Local 202, of the International Brotherhood of Teamsters, etc., were indicted for extortion. Nine officials of these two unions, were later convicted including several merchants and owners. Five minor perjury and one important forgery case in these "labor union front" rackets were later prosecuted. The Manganaro case in the trucking of fruits and other perishables, along with the Waldorf trucking case, are examples. Both have already been discussed at length. These set the pattern for the 1990's successful special Federal racket prosecutions in the sensitive food and fruit industries.

Another pattern example of an important 1938 investigation against union officials, and corrupt business was the one against a group of electrical contractors accused of organized, collusive bidding on both private and public contracts! That particular investigation dealt with the electrical construction industries of the building trades. Other important investigations leading directly to indictments of leaders of important rackets and often officials, and police themselves, were: the taxicab investigation in the transportation industries; a markets

investigation in the food industries and an
investigation of newsstand rackets! In the 1990's
Mayor Dinkins created the Mollen Commission to
specially and independently investigate Police
drug corruption, etc. Two other less extensive
city prosecutions, involving officials, was the
Spector contempt case (the only contempt case
which was later reversed in the Court of Appeals
for the Appellant) and that Federal conviction of
the impeached Judge Manton! Prosecution of
officials in rackets cases who often had political
connections made the Dewey "time bomb" method of
the 1930's always particularly effective.

The year 1939 represented an unusual
concentration in the fields of industrial labor
racketeering in all industries. Besides those
already mentioned along with the perjury and
contempt cases which followed them, the rackets
prosecutors broke a particularly vicious group of
labor racket officials. These racketeering Labor
Union officials, of Local 150 of the Needle
Industry Union, had formed a conspiracy to
intimidate workers and employers mainly by means
of the "school for sabotage," (which we have
already noted in the clothing industries where
their acid and machinery damaging technique had
proved exceedingly lucrative.) The "teachings" of

that school for sabotage also taught the current prosecutor's some of today's racket busting techniques!

Another "time bomb" pattern case of a labor union official in the building trades was broken in 1939 with the investigation of the Cement Masons Union, Local 750, in which the Secretary-Treasurer was indicted for grand larceny of the Union's funds. The evidence the Rackets Bureau piled up in several of these later industrial racketeering cases was so sure-fire that the defendants pleaded guilty in several cases to the first degree charge! These 1939 racket cases all show clearly the general pattern above described for the effective legal prosecution of later organized racketeering upon the vital New York City Bureau's and Departments; especially in the municipal trucking, building, and City vehicles groups. It is a picture perfect pattern of how best these recurring rackets are still being repeated in the 1990's.

Perhaps the most important case of the year 1940 was another which has been "followed" and used as a model case from the Dewey Special Investigation most recently in 1992. This was the 1930's indictment of George Scalise, an important building trades racketeer with widespread underworld connections, who had operated a tremendous racket with a legal "front" in the building trades for a long number of years. He had become the president of a great international union, Building Service Employees International Union, due to the tremendous wealth and power he had massed through his building trades racketeering against New York City's labor, and labor unions. With the "time Bomb" investigation technique, Scalise was sentenced to serve a jail term of from ten to twenty years. He found it wiser to also plead guilty to additional charges of Federal tax evasion for 3 1/2 years upon the completion of his original racketeering jail term.

The New York County Rackets Bureau during 1940 also was able by vigorous investigation to return large sums of money to be paid by way of back taxes to the City, State and Federal governments from several of the racketeer "industrialists" under income tax law. As a result of Rackets Bureau prosecutions minor racketeering against honest labor unions was also especially investigated. Several union officials were indicted and convicted of grand larceny and extortion against labor unions in connection therewith. A ring-leader in the sabotage set-up against labor unions and business named Mary

Ottone, was also convicted in the 1940's for her activities in property racketeering! The late 1940's showed that the former widespread destruction of property that previously accompanied the City's industrial disputes was no longer as prevalent as it had been. Widespread vandalism in such disputes was the subject of vigorous attack by the Rackets Bureau during the 1940's in cooperation with the Police Department and the result then became most gratifying. For example, in connection with the union painter's strike of 1939, the immediate intervention of the Rackets Bureau resulted in the restraining of several of the main racket perpetrators. Industrial vandálism due to racketeering reached a low ebb by the late 1940's. Unfortunately the rackets "cycle" recurred in the same patterns in 1960's and resulted in the RICO Act of 1970, as amended. There has been a new pattern of racket recurrence against honest labor unions and honest business in the 1990's. RICO is working well and much used. Again officials of both government and unions are involved.

The brazen perjury committed by witnesses continues in 1990 and was also the object of strenuous prosecution by the Rackets Bureau during 1940. Contempt was then one of the main tools for effective witness help in anti-racketeering law enforcement. Witnesses will forever continue to lie and commit perjury. As we have seen above in many cases, perjury by witnesses and contempt convictions and perjury by defendants is most often induced by fear and threats or by a fearful loyalty to the racket bosses involved. As a result the New York County Rackets Bureau started the treatment of perjury by witnesses as a major long-scale necessity. That continues in the 1990's. For example, Samuel Hiat of the above "School for Sabotage" in 1939 was convicted of "subordination of perjury" when he had been picked as one of the principal witnesses for the prosecution of that "School for Sabotage" case. Subordination of perjury is surprisingly however not so frequent in the late 1990's cases, because Judges today treat perjury very strictly, and rightly so.

The Scalise case investigation of 1930's also lead the Rackets Bureau to make a house cleaning against union officials in the building industries with the indictment of four officials of Local 32B of the B.S.E.I.U. These officials were: Robert Conroy, Frank Gold, Manuel Saverino, and Joseph Polotnick, all charged with <u>extortion from</u> <u>employees</u> who had been compelled to deal with their union. Finally, during 1940, another key-trucking situation, was quickly investigated and prosecuted by the "time bomb" prosecution methods. It was a conspiracy to extort money from the grocery chain of H. C. Bohack Co., by William Campbell, formerly a labor delegate of Local 807 of the International Brotherhood of Teamsters. With him, Abe Kittay and Irving Dworetsky, then a fugitive, were found and indicted and brought to justice. Now the RICO Act of 1970, as amended, has been instrumental in curbing at early stages some of the building industry and extortion rackets of the 1990's.

These are the major "time bomb" investigations and prosecutions patterns of organized racketeering now more concerned with white collar, computer, and industrial, and securities rackets. It must be remembered, however, that the application of successful "time bomb" investigation and prosecution against recurring racketeering is not by any means as simple as this summary may tend to make it appear. There is a powerful political or budget crunch "opposition" to be overcome; not only in terms of independent investigation and prosecution work, but also in case selection. There remains political pressures, to which the Federal, State and City rackets work must continue to remain quite independent!

These are the factors which formerly hamstrung the work of the prosecutors assigned to racket prosecutions case selection and trial before the "model" New York County Rackets Bureau was established in 1938! Today such pressures only serve to drive the young men of the Federal, State, and City rackets work further in their determination to keep all the major cities' industrial and union structures free of racketeering, and case prosecution selection independent of politics.

Now in the 1990's some 50 years after this dedicated team of hard working lawyers under the able guidance of Tom Dewey labored to turn our City away from organized criminal rackets, what is the result? The answer is in the 1990's that almost all labor unions are no longer racket controlled. A few organized large international rackets actively operate, largely in drugs, gambling, and money laundering. In 1993 and 1994 the large increase of illegal immigrants has caused vigorous Federal and State racket prosecutions, and tough border restrictions and prosecutions working on, not for, these illegal rackets involving immigration.

New York in 1993 is a different City from what is was in the late 1930's. Many U.S. States are heavily strained to assist legal and illegal immigrants already here. Waves of immigrants largely blacks, hispanics, and chinese, for example, have changed the ethnic population balance of New York City. White people are no longer a New York City majority! New and more powerful unions, computers for immigration and security, and communications, have changed the way all industrial and civic business is done; and people are taxed and recorded - mostly for the better, some for the worse.

For example, New York was in the late 1930's a thriving seaport, with strong seamen's and dock workers unions. It is no longer! New York still has empty piers stretching into the Hudson and the East River. This is partly due to the advent of container ships and to the agreement that many longshoremen must be paid for each ship that is unloaded whether they work or not. That is legal. In its place we have much increased airport crime and drug related rackets.

There is also the perception that the Port of New York and New York City is too expensive to mount conventions and trade fairs because elaborate rules prevent an exhibiter even changing a light bulb for himself. Consider the New York Flower Show. It was once forced to leave the New York Coliseum because truckers threatened to leave the fragile plants on the sidewalk exposed to the cold March wind, unless further moneys were paid them! Whether this was fairly done or racketeering is unknown. It was not prosecuted. The New York garden show has finally recurred on a much smaller scale on one of the newer rebuilt piers.

Major trade cities will always attract some rackets in a repetitive similar type criminal pattern to the 1930's. Now the recurring disclosure of racketeering publicity and daily criminal media news hampers the effort to continue New York as a great world trade and convention town in the 1990's. But the New York newspapers almost daily continue to sell newspapers by such "news." However, with stringent licensing of vendors and newsstands and street kiosks for transportation, as well as the New York City transit police, New York city has shown improvement from the minor rackets in the 1990's. Auto theft rates and auto "stripping" by gangs remains a current problem, for many cities, internationally. Perhaps NAFTA and freer trade in auto's will further help to stop this trend, especially in large port cities.

Considering the 1990's new extensive anti-rackets laws like RICO and the "time bomb" prosecutorial type work of the F.B.I. and U.S. attorneys, anti-rackets work <u>cooperation</u> cannot be over-emphasized. The U.S. Department of Justice, and F.B.I. is gearing up for an expected increase in 1994 in crime and racket cases partly due to the world-wide continued recession with new guidelines for prosecutions. The old Rackets Bureau "time bomb" prosecution and trial patterns remain and are much used.

The U.S. Congress has passed new amendments to <u>money laundering</u> statutes targeting also financial institutions. Financial markets, with computers, have greatly expanded in the 1990's. Recognizing the broad scope of the Federal money laundering statutes, the Department of Justice instituted changes in its guidelines for money laundering and drug prosecutions under 18 USC 981-982, Ch. 1956-7. These are the money laundering and property forfeitures sections. The U.S. Justice Department now has a separate Money Laundering Section established in its Criminal Division to ensure consistency in certain types of racket prosecutions; and to now assist prosecutors in the formulation and prosecution of increasing money laundering cases! The needed independent prosecution case selection shown in the 1930's, has reappeared in the 1990's, in the U.S. Government. These amended criminal guidelines acknowledge that the current problems in applying the money laundering racket proceeds statutes are greater than the problems that ordinarily arise when a new criminal statute is applied for the first time. "Money laundering" racketeering thus now applies to everything from the international transfer by wire of hundreds of millions of dollars in drug proceeds confiscated in New York banks, to the purchase of an automobile with funds computer "robbed" from a bank.

The amended federal guidelines require federal prosecutors to get approval of the Justice Department Money Laundering Section before instituting certain racket prosecutions! Add these to new "consultation" requirements for certain types of cases which set forth new reporting requirements for prosecutors in money laundering cases. These cases are often also large forfeiture cases. Often in 1993 and 1994 we see whole pages of forfeitures and sales of cars, boats, property, and accounts by U.S. authorities.

However money and property forfeitures have

proved a great detriment to the drug and money laundering rackets. The purpose of these guidelines, and of the Money Laundering Section itself, is to "provide a means to ensure the orderly development of the case law and to assist prosecutors in applying these statutes at a time when the case law in this area is developing very fast."

In addition, the U.S. Justice Department acknowledges that the civil forfeiture statute for money laundering gives the government a good means to forfeit property involved in a wide range of racket offenses especially where illegal money is the principal purpose and for which forfeiture is not otherwise provided. Examples are fraud, environmental crime or public corruption. By alleging that the money proceeds of certain racket crimes were "laundered," the government can obtain forfeiture of the property as well as of any property used to facilitate the crime! Recognizing the breadth and magnitude of this new racket prosecution power, the prosecutors acknowledge that: "[w]e must use these powerful weapons carefully." RICO and this new forfeiture power will greatly aid criminal racket prosecution cases in the 1990's, when added to the proven successful old Rackets Bureau "time bomb" investigation methods.

No description in words, can ever demonstrate one factor which is undoubtedly an important key to the present success in the 1990's of the difficult, legal, criminal prosecution work in which the cooperating rackets prosecutors are daily engaged, under tremendous pressure. This factor is the spirit and drive to be again of real service to the public in protecting citizens and industries from racketeering in any form, or the effects thereof. Undoubtedly, this spirit underlying the efficient detective and agent investigations, and Court prosecutions set-up by the New York County Racket's Bureau and the District Attorney's offices in the 1930's and 1940's will live on for many years.

We have seen the 1930's and 1940's "rip-offs" through a couple of months of Mr. & Mrs. John New Yorker's average family city life. They felt the costly rackets in simply pursuing the ordinary course and necessities of daily living, in their costs of basic living without really being aware of them. Exactly so, today in the 1990's. This clearly reveals the 1990's _importance_ and necessity for new timely electronic means, and new laws for active, independent, Federal, State, and

City organized anti-crime <u>cooperation</u>! For budget economy reasons some would like to contend that the racket cases ought to be handled by the regular Federal, State, and City District Attorney's staffs, etc! By experience that this simply does not work due to the needed special pattern of "time bomb" handling of an organized racket investigation, indictment, trial and subsequent appeals, be it local, national or international. Foolish government economy could cause us to repeat the unsuccessful uncoordinated prosecutions <u>prior</u> to the 1930's! The Dewey "time Bomb" racket investigations and coordinated prosecution methods must be carefully followed for the 1990's decade for the benefit of all people, especially with legal and illegal gambling on the increase world wide. History does repeat itself.

The New York Rackets Bureau, which Mr. Dewey created and founded under Mr. Gurfein on January 1, 1938 as a division of the New York County District Attorney's Office, after the Dewey Special Investigation, clearly did more to sweep <u>rackets</u> out of New York City than any other prosecuting agency New York or any other City, has ever known. It stopped then the New York racketeers exactions of millions of dollars, of its political protection; and of its legitimate and illegitimate labor "front." It is a successful historical model, not to be forgotten, and to be used now.

If our friends, the New Yorker family, could realize something of the character, difficulty and extent of this work, every New York City consumer who simply believed in pursuing a quiet every day working, democratic life, would be eternally grateful to every one of those inspired young men; who in the 1930's and 1940's set the rackets busting pattern for future racket prosecutions.

Let's keep New York City's racketeer parasites and international racketeers out of your pocket and mine, today, and tomorrow. The costs-of-living and taxes, are high enough for all peoples, worldwide, without racketeering.

Mollen Panel to Recommend Permanent Corruption Body

Independent Monitor of Police Misconduct

By SELWYN RAAB

A mayoral panel on police corruption will recommend today the creation of a permanent independent agency to monitor police misconduct, New York City officials said yesterday.

The officials said the panel, known as the Mollen Commission, will recommend that the new body have subpoena power and the authority to conduct its own investigations of graft and misconduct in the city's 30,000-member Police Department. The agency would act as an oversight body to scrutinize the department's internal methods for investigating and deterring graft and other abuses, according to the officials.

But they said the new agency — with five unpaid commissioners and a paid staff of lawyers and investigators — would not have the power to prosecute criminal cases; that would remain the responsibility of local district attorneys or Federal prosecutors.

The officials, who spoke on the condition of anonymity, said they had been advised of the principal findings of an interim report that will be released today.

But it is unclear whether Mayor-elect Rudolph W. Giuliani is likely to endorse any of the recommendations made by the Mollen Commission, which was appointed by Mayor David N. Dinkins. Mr. Giuliani has said that he favored a special prosecutor to root out police corruption.

Milton Mollen, the chairman of the panel, said that the report was delivered yesterday to Mr. Dinkins and to Mr. Giuliani, whose term begins on Saturday. A final, more extensive report will be given to Mr. Giuliani in April or May, Mr. Mollen said.

A spokesman for Mayor Dinkins said yesterday that the Mollen Commission's report today would include findings that some delegates of the Patrolmen's Benevolent Association, the main police union, may have attempted to block corruption investigations.

'Particularly Disturbed'

Leland T. Jones, Mr. Dinkins's press secretary, said last night that the Mayor was "particularly disturbed" by a finding in the preliminary report that "a variety of sources including police officers have reported that police unions helped perpetuate the characteristics of a police culture that fosters corruption."

Mr. Jones said Mr. Dinkins "in particular was disturbed that the commission learned that delegates of the P.B.A. have attempted to thwart law-enforcement efforts into police corruption." Mr. Jones declined to be more specific about the findings, saying that he had not read the report, but that Mr. Dinkins had said his comments about the union stemmed from assertions by the commission.

Relations between the P.B.A. and Mayor Dinkins have been strained for some time. The P.B.A. actively campaigned for Mr. Giuliani during the mayoral race, not only endorsing him but running ads supporting him and attacking Mr. Dinkins.

Mr. Mollen and the four other members of the commission declined yesterday to discuss the report. The panel was appointed by Mr. Dinkins in the summer of 1992 after six city police officers were arrested in Suffolk County on cocaine-trafficking charges.

At hearings last October, the commission heard testimony from admitted former rogue officers of how separate bands of officers robbed drug dealers, offered protection to other dealers and assaulted innocent residents in poor and crime-ridden neighborhoods.

At the close of the hearings, all the commission members suggested they supported creating an independent body or auditor to oversee the department's internal system for fighting corruption, but they did not specify how the unit should function.

It was unclear yesterday if Mr. Giuliani would support the commission's concept of a permanent review agency. Officials said the commission rejected the establishment of an inspector general or a special prosecutor to oversee the anti-corruption efforts.

Mr. Giuliani, a former Federal prosecutor who supervised many police and other corruption cases, said during the mayoral race that he favored re-creating the office of a special state prosecutor to investigate police corruption. The special prosecutor's post, which was established in 1973 as a temporary office after a previous police corruption scandal, was abolished in 1990 by Gov. Mario M. Cuomo and the Legislature.

Last week, aides to Mr. Giuliani, who spoke only on the condition of anonymity, said it was unlikely that he would fully accept the proposals of a commission that is in effect is a lame-duck group appointed by a lame-duck Mayor.